Witch Hill.

See page 15.

WITCH HILL:

A HISTORY OF SALEM WITCHCRAFT.

INCLUDING

ILLUSTRATIVE SKETCHES OF PERSONS AND PLACES.

BY REV. Z. A. MUDGE,

AUTHOR OF "VIEWS FROM PLYMOUTH ROCK," "FOREST BOY," "THE CHRISTIAN STATESMAN," ETC., ETC.

THREE ILLUSTRATIONS.

NEW YORK:
CARLTON & LANAHAN.
SAN FRANCISCO: E. THOMAS.
CINCINNATI: HITCHCOCK & WALDEN.
SUNDAY-SCHOOL DEPARTMENT.

PREFACE

WE have examined, in preparing the material for this volume, "Woodward's Records of Salem Witchcraft, copied from the Original Documents;" "Hutchinson's History of Massachusetts;" Cotton Mather's "Wonders of the Invisible World;" Calef's "More Wonders of the Invisible World;" Mather's "Magnolia;" "Salem Witchcraft," by the Hon. C. W. Upham; The "Mather Papers;" "Cotton Mather and Salem Witchcraft," in the "North American Review" for April, 1869; and "Salem Witchcraft and Cotton Mather," in the "Historical Magazine" for September and October, 1869. Some works less frequently used are referred to in the body of the volume.

Our search into the original sources, so far as they have been within our reach, has been chiefly valuable for the assurance that it has given us that there is very little indeed to reward such pains-taking not found in Mr. Upham's writings. His two volumes and his *résumé* in the Historical Magazine make a thesaurus on the subject.

Views from "Witch Hill" present some painful,

and much somber scenery; and if it had been our province to make rather than exhibit views, we should have endeavored to entertain the reader with pleasanter pictures. As it is, we think they will be found interesting, and know they will be profitable if read thoughtfully. The lesson they teach lies on the surface of the story, and is adapted to the correction of dangerous current errors. Our prayer is that it may be owned of God to that end.

The illustrations in this volume are taken from Upham's "Salem Witchcraft" by the kind permission of the author.

CHAPTER I.

THE LOCALITY OF OUR STORY.

CHAPTER II.

PORTRAITS OF NOTABLE PERSONS.

CHAPTER III.

THE BEGINNING OF STRIFE.

CHAPTER IV.

THE FLOCK AND THE SHEPHERDS.

CHAPTER IX.

THE ACCUSERS STRIKE HIGHER.

CHAPTER X.

AN EXCELLENT MATRON.

CHAPTER XI.

THE VOICE OF THE WATCHMEN.

CHAPTER XII.

A CHANGE OF BASE.

CHAPTER XIII.

MARKED CASES.

CHAPTER XIV.

A REVEREND ELDER.

CHAPTER XV.

THE JACOBS FAMILY.

CHAPTER XVI.

CURIOUS BUT SAD.

CHAPTER XVII.

THE CHRIST-LIKE SPIRIT.

CHAPTER XVIII.

STATEMENTS OF PERSONAL SUFFERERS.

CHAPTER XIX.

THE SPECIAL COURT.

CHAPTER XX.

A FATAL RESULT, AND A PAUSE.

CHAPTER XXV.

THE COLLAPSE.

CHAPTER XXVI.

INCIDENTS OF THE TRIALS AND EXECUTIONS.

CHAPTER XXVII.

AN IMPORTANT INQUIRY.

CHAPTER XXVIII.

COURT SCENES AND THE JUDGES.

CHAPTER XXIX.

"THE POOR AFFLICTED."

CHAPTER XXX.

PENITENTIAL TEARS.

CHAPTER XXXI.

A VISIT TO THE HISTORIC LOCALITIES.

Illustrations.

WITCH HILL.

CHAPTER I.

The Locality of our Story.

A PLEASANT ride on the Eastern Railroad for about three fourths of an hour will bring us from Boston to the city of Salem. In the witchcraft period this place included what is now the town of Peabody, lying on its northern boundary, called then the "Middle Precinct," and Danvers, known as Salem Village, situated still further north.

Every well-informed grammar school boy of our country knows Salem as one of the prominent cities of New England. If a visit were made to it, and to the towns once included within its territory, there would be seen all the peculiarities of New England scenery, and of a first-class New England community. Here are churches, common schools, literary institutions, commerce and manufactories, all in intense activity. Let us take our stand on one of the many rocky eminences which command a view of a large portion of this region—on Witch Hill itself.* Let us remove the railroads, stop the

* See Frontispiece.

clatter of steam factories, change all the vessels whose sails whiten the extended line of sea into canoes, a few ships, and smaller craft of a queer construction. Let us take away the great mass of the dwellings and their population, leaving a scattered settlement in houses usually humble. Let us fill most of the land with craggy rocks, and forests through which a few rough roads have been cut, and, in vision, put Puritans of the original type in the place of the present Yankee inhabitants. Then we shall see things in a measure as they were nearly two hundred years ago. Into the midst of such scenes, and to such a people, we shall endeavor to introduce our readers. To feel justly the effect of the stirring incidents with which they are to be made acquainted, they will need to know something of the locality; to understand the strange conduct of the prominent actors in our tragedy, it will be necessary to know the community of which they made a part, and the times in which they lived.

The witchcraft delusion of Salem occurred in 1692. The first permanent settlement of the place was made in 1628. John Endicott, who came with the first immigrants, and was the first Governor of the colony, was a man of great business abilities, and, though not free from evident infirmities, possessed a genuine Christian heart. He planned and executed liberal things for his own and future generations. Under his management, and that of the governors who immediately followed him, a very wise policy was adopted to induce settlers in the New World to select this locality, and to secure an intelligent, moral, and thrifty community.

Their land policy was admirable. They gave extensive tracts of country to rich men of known enterprise and excellence of character, who expended large sums in opening roads, clearing farms, erecting the necessary buildings, introducing domestic animals, implements of agriculture, and the best varieties of fruits and vegetables; in doing this they necessarily opened the way for and encouraged all the mechanic arts. Grants were made on condition that special enterprises should be carried on. One man received lands for "setting up plowing," and so the first plows were introduced. Another started "salt-works" through the same kind of encouragement. We shall become acquainted in the course of our history with some of these large, wealthy land-holders.

But if the land grants had been confined to these rich men, notwithstanding they were usually men of a generous policy toward their laborers, the final results would have been bad. Labor and thrift were wisely considered the best of wealth. Men who were penniless on the other side of the Atlantic came over, and, first working out the price of their passage on lands given or leased at a low rent, then working out from the forest farms and homes of their own, they became prominent actors in both State and Church. With these yeomen we shall become quite intimate. Of course the work to be done, the sacrifices to be made, and the energy to be put forth by all classes, was immense. The forests were to be cleared, roads to be opened, the wild beasts of the forest to be conquered, and the Indians to be watched, fought, and governed. Then their own government needed to be conformed to the peculiar necessities of a growing country, for which no old model would answer. Lastly, not last, but foremost in their thoughts and hearts, religion and education were to be established together and every-where exalted.

The farmers at first opened roads to their own lands—rocky and "stumpy" no doubt, for many years. The first road made by the common labor was that to the meeting-house.

The mode of travel was for a long time, if by land, on horseback. It would be curious now to see the men, women, and children, often two or three persons on one animal, thus picking their way to town or to church.

But much of the travel and transportation of goods was by canoes. These were of two kinds: those made of white pine logs, scooped out and shaped for the purpose, and those made of bark in the Indian manner. These last were best for most purposes, if managed with an Indian's skill. They skimmed along the shore with ease, slipping up the shallowest water of the beaches and creeks, and even ventured into the rough seas round the headlands; then, furthermore, they were easily borne on a man's head across necks of land to be launched on the other side.

So important to the welfare of the whole people

did the Salem fathers deem the canoe fleet, that they appointed a board of their best men as canoe inspectors. The fourth day of May was canoe day. By nine o'clock in the morning, at specified points on the North and South rivers—arms of the sea north and south of the strip of land on which their town was situated—all the canoes of the settlement were to appear. After serious and faithful inspection, they received, if judged worthy, the official seal, without which any canoe was liable to a fine of ten shillings. Mr. Upham suggests that this occasion was the first Fourth of July ever celebrated in America. We have no doubt that if Young America was then in the country (and we shall have occasion to show that he came over very early) there was severe testing of the relative fleetness of canoes, and skill and strength of arms in propelling them, as well as courage in urging them over the surging seas. There were no fire-crackers, and powder was too valuable to be burned for the sake of its noisy explosion; but the young people, then as now, had lusty voices, and knew how to make them ring along the echoing shores in loud shouts and merry laughter.

Canoe Day was not the only occasion on which the fathers of the locality and their families enjoyed hearty, innocent recreation. When a neighbor had cut his timber and hewed it into a frame for a house, brought all his materials to the spot and put them in readiness, then the country was astir for "a raising." It was a "good turn" rendered freely in expectation that under the same circumstances it would be reciprocated. What lifting, and shouting, and general confusion there was to get the frame of a small house into place! while now a first-class church is erected without disturbing the sick across the street, and without the labor of any except a few mechanics and their powerful machinery.

The huskings were, however, much greater, because more general and regularly occurring occasions for merriment. The huge piles of golden grain, the result of a summer's toil; the men and women gathering about it in their "homespun" clothes—the old folks with relaxed gravity and the young folks sparkling with wit and overflowing with gladness; and the "farmer's supper" in the great kitchen which followed, made an occasion remembered with pleasure by all.

Then there were the winter evenings, long and quiet, (not as now, short and bustling,) when the snow-storms of New England were not, as in these degenerate days, windy pretensions, whose snow a few steam-plows put into inglorious heaps by the wayside, or a day's sun melts; but furious tempests, and earnest blockades of men and animals for weeks. It was then that the fire blazed cheerfully in the ample fire-place. The huge logs gave assurance that winter might knock with his iciest fingers, and yet not be admitted. The children and domestics in their seats against the jambs, and the older people on the settees before the fire, told their stories, read over and over their few books, sang their evening songs, offered their evening prayers, and were early in beds where sleep was too sound and refreshing for dreams.

The first settlers of Salem found no Indians living in their immediate vicinity, though savage assaults upon the white people sometimes occurred not far from them. Having, therefore, no Indian drones in their midst, they determined to have no white ones. They allowed no strangers to remain among them without "a license," and stringent laws were made against Sabbath-breaking, drunkenness, swearing, and such wicked practices. Two boys among some new comers behaved badly, and were sent back to England! We fear it would make a scattering now in most of the villages of the country if all the bad boys were ordered across the sea!

Though the fathers in this vicinity were thus jealous of the good morals of their colony they unwisely introduced alcohol, the worst enemy of morality. Governor Winthrop, writing to his son in 1648, says: "They are all well in Salem, and your uncle is now beginning to distill." Beyond a doubt many were ill, and grew rapidly worse from that moment.

A better business than distilling was early commenced. Bentley, a Salem historian, says: "In 1636 they built at Marble Harbor, then Salem, a vessel of 120 tons. This ship, called the Desire, was commanded by Captain Peirce, who made the first almanac ever published in America. This he was induced to prepare after the arrival of Glover's printing-press, which was afterward established at Cambridge. In Salem, 1640, they built a ship of 300 tons, and in 1641 she was launched."

Ship owning at once became profitable, for he adds concerning the next ship which was built, "she made eighty per cent. profit the same year."

The school-master was soon abroad in Salem, notwithstanding the common idea of the ignorance of its people in the witchcraft matter. There was a grammar school teacher in Salem in 1637, a graduate of Cambridge University in England, who prepared for admission a part of the first class of Harvard College. He was immediately succeeded by equally competent teachers, so that the town from the first afforded the means of a preparatory classical training to its sons. This was occasioned in part, no doubt, from a fact which the reader will need to remember, namely, that most of the considerable land-holders around Salem owned "town lots" and had residences in town. This was favorable, of course, to their social, educational, and religious development. "The farmers" in and about Salem Village did not see the school-master so early nor so frequently, but they sought, as far as their circumstances allowed, his important services. One of their number, who had more than the average knowledge of "writing, ciphering, and spelling," was employed to receive his neighbors' children at stated times at his own house for instruction in these branches. An itinerating school and school-master were sustained at one time. Thus was cradled in Salem Village and its kindred settlements the New England common school system.

The fathers of Salem devised liberal things in all great enterprises. A favorite object with them until 1642 was to make their town the capital of New England. They schemed to locate the proposed college in their vicinity, and made a reserve of lands on the Marblehead farms for this purpose. But the college went to Cambridge, and Boston became the commercial center. It may sound strangely now to name the Marblehead farms in connection with the oldest of the eminent seats of learning in America; but the bracing air and the grand views connected with that locality make it, in point of scenery and health, far superior to the one chosen.

The military spirit of Salem, but more especially of Salem Village, was one of its most prominent peculiarities. Fear of the Indians had been its occasion and inspiration. A company was early formed in the Village, and the adults who were able to bear arms, whether rich or poor, old or young, joined it. We shall meet in the witchcraft proceedings men who belonged to it, and had seen service in the fiercest fights of the famous Narragansett War. In fact, Salem has been, from its first settlement, eminently military. It has given men of distinction to every war of the country, not excepting that of the Great Rebellion. The best known of these heroes, though perhaps not the greatest, was General Israel Putnam, whose wolf exploit in Connecticut and cool daring on

Bunker Hill are among the facts of history first learned by American school-children.

The village company was officered by its most prominent men, and there were no honors more highly prized than those it conferred. To be even a corporal in it was to be known as "Corporal" the rest of one's life. Grave deacons, dignified justices, and the aristocratic land-holder, did not feel degraded to train in its ranks, and were proud of its commissions. It met for drill on the grounds made sacred by the Sabbath gatherings for worship, and was composed of the same men who constituted the Church and sustained its interest. One of the *practices*, if not one of the duties, of the captain was, before dismissing his company, to give notice of Church or parish meetings, and, no doubt, the drill was often immediately followed by the spiritual exercises of God's house.

A horse company was also made up in part from the village.

In religion the Salem people were of the "straitest sect" of our Puritan fathers. Their convictions on this subject were very deep, and held with greater tenacity than life. Nor do we find them mere bigots. Their perception of the essential requirements for salvation were clearly scriptural, and their experience of the power of Gospel truth was generally a fact of their daily lives. Greatly mistaken in some grave matters they certainly were. They had sought out this "corner of the earth," at great peril and sacrifice, to build up political and religious freedom for themselves.

They desired those who differed from them to seek some other corner. How many corners God would have to provide on this earth if every party in politics and every sect in religion should seek one for itself, and what "border wars" there would be!

With a portion of this people, whose history and training we have thus briefly sketched, we are to become acquainted at a period when the elements of their character were so intensely fired that they shook their social fabric, as the volcano shakes the mount from which it issues.

CHAPTER II.

Portraits of Notable Persons.

THE time intervening between the landing of the first settlers in Salem, in 1628, and the witchcraft tragedy, was only about sixty-four years. Some of the earliest notable men had not been gone many years from the active scenes of the settlement, and a few of the fathers of the second generation who had received the immediate mantle of the first were still alive. Thus the facts which we have narrated had an immediate bearing upon the transactions of our story.

Many eminent men and characters of rare originality were produced in this vicinity during these two generations. Indeed, no section of the country, it may be safely affirmed, has produced more men whose names have become national than that included within the limits of our history. But we purpose to present to the reader the portraits of those faces only which will appear with more or less prominence in subsequent scenes. To appreciate their part on the stage we shall need to know them behind the curtain.

Whatever turn our story takes, the *Putnams* generally appear in some relation to it. There were three brothers, Thomas, Nathaniel, and John, sons of the first immigrant of the name. Their father owned large tracts of forest to the north of the village, and was a man of energy and thrift. He left to his eldest son, Thomas, after the English custom, the largest portion of his substance, but gave to all valuable property. They were men, as we shall see, distinguished by sharp lines of character, great capacity for business, and marked executive power. As Thomas died before 1692, we shall know him only in his sons, *Thomas*, *Edward*, and *Joseph*. The first will be spoken of as Sergeant Thomas, clerk of the parish, and will be constantly upon or flitting across the stage; his wife Ann and daughter Ann, their wild, expressive countenances looking as if they saw John's vision of Michael and his angels, fighting with the Great Red Dragon and his angels, can never be forgotten when once seen. Edward became Deacon Edward, whose genuine piety and generally sound judgment were overborne by the frenzied excitement of the delusion, but who lived to see his fellows, not as trees nor as "specters," but as men walking. Joseph was the son of his father's second wife, who was living as a widow on the homestead in 1692, a mile and a quarter north-west of the village. Joseph was just married then, and a young man. He will not come upon the stage often during the acting of our tragi-comedy, but when he does it will be with a flashing eye, and an outstretched, defiant right arm. We shall always be glad to see him. He was the father of "Old Put" of the Revolution, who inherited his towering bravery.

Nathaniel Putnam was a man of wealth, obtained by his wife, as well as by inheritance and thrift; he was known as landlord Putnam. He was prominent in all political and Church matters, of great energy and influence. He will appear early in the witchcraft scenes, but seems to have had prudence as well as force, and so was not so painfully connected with them as some others. He lived, where his descendants have lived to this day, about a mile south-east of the old church of the Village.

John Putnam, known as "Lieutenant," and later as "Captain," was neither less energetic nor prominent than his older brothers, Thomas and Nathaniel, though somewhat less discreet. There is something honest and straightforward expressed in his open countenance and military air. He has fought the Pequod Indians, and you cannot help feeling assured that fighting for what he feels to be the right is not difficult for him. You would not suspect him of a mean transaction, though we may have to prove one such against him. At any rate trickery and concealment are no parts of his character. His face will become perfectly familiar.

These three Putnam brothers had large families, high position, and great influence. If they had been clannish they might well-nigh have ruled Salem Village. But they were remarkable for their individuality, often acting independent of and even in opposition to each other. They all had town residences besides rural homes, and so were brought in contact with kindred leading minds. So, too, they all followed the practice of other land-holders, and gave to their sons, as they became heads of families, farms out of their own estates, thus developing their land and strengthening the family influence. Another practice should be remembered: each son learned some useful trade, so that the farmers were carpenters, masons, blacksmiths, etc.

Here is the portrait of one whom we shall love to see often: he is *Corporal Ingersall;* for, having risen to that rank in the Village company, the honor clung to him for life. Even the title "Deacon," which he bore about fifty years, could not overshadow it. He settled in early manhood in the Village near where the first meeting-house was built. His house was a large one for the times, one room especially so. This room seems to have been devised, out of the largeness of his heart, for the benefit of the public, and particularly for the parish and Church. At any rate it was subsequently turned to that account. The religious pioneers of this Continent have every-where, and in every generation, found the ample kitchen of a whole-hearted brother a most convenient place. It was so with Salem Village parish and Church. When a wintry Sabbath proved unusually severe, and but few assembled in the unwarmed meeting-house, an adjournment to Deacon Ingersall's warm "great room" was a common expedient. There were no "lecture rooms," "vestries," nor "chapels" of course, and the "parish committee" met at the Deacon's; the "weekly lecture" was often given there; and for "the Church meeting" it was found a more comfortable place than the cold meeting-house. In fact, the "great room" was a very great convenience, and the Deacon's face was never turned coldly to his brethren however often or in whatever numbers they came.

Deacon Ingersall was one of those interesting characters, found among most of the new settlements of our country, for whom the lawyer has been unhappily substituted. He was the "referee" in the settlement of perplexing business matters, the umpire in differences, the "go-between" in his neighbors' quarrels; and all bowed to the majesty of his good sense, clear judgment, and fearless integrity. He owned seventy-five acres in the center of the Village, and was never wealthy in comparison with the most of his associates; but what he lacked in estate he made up in wealth of character. He married a Lynn woman of like spirit, and, though they had no children who lived, all the children of the parish lived in their hearts. His house had become by his generous spirit so common to all, and being on the traveled road to the farms north and west, he was licensed to keep "an ordinary," that is, a place of entertainment. We shall become more familiar with him and his large room.

The next person to whom we would introduce our readers is *Francis Nurse.* He was a man less John-like in his disposition than Deacon Ingersall, and of humbler social rank and influence, as he seems never to have been even "corporal" in military life, nor an office-bearer in the Church; yet he possessed a well-earned "good name," which "is better than great riches." He too was "umpire," "referee," an arbiter of conflicting claims, and an adjuster of disputed boundary lines among his neighbors. He lived for forty years, before becoming of historic note, in Salem town, just out of the settlement, on the North River, toward Beverly Ferry. He was during this period a "tray-maker." His wife (we greet her now with cheerfulness and respect, but shall part with her in pity, love, and tears) belonged to an excellent family by the name of Town, other members of which we shall meet. Francis Nurse and Rebecca, his wife, had four sons, Samuel, John, Francis, and Benjamin; and four daughters: Rebecca, who became the wife of Thomas Preston; Mary, wife of John Tarbell; Elizabeth, wife of William Russell; and Sarah, unmarried during the period of our history.

Nurse was fifty-eight years of age, and his wife fifty-seven, when they entered upon an enterprise requiring the energy and faith of youth, and the wisdom and prudence of age. He purchased of the Rev. James Allen, one of the ministers of the First Church, in Boston, a three-hundred-acre tract of land, with its mansion, out-buildings, and partial cultivation, known as "The Townsend Bishop Farm." The price agreed upon was four hundred pounds sterling, not less certainly than twenty-five hundred dollars of the present currency—a great sum, "a fortune" in fact, for those days. But he did not pay one penny down, and seems to have had but little with which to pay. The terms were peculiar, shrewd, and, what is perhaps the most remarkable feature of them, very favorable *for both parties.* Twenty years were given him in which to pay it. But Nurse, his sons, sons-in-law, and their wives—for credit seems justly due to every one of them—were equal to the daring enterprise. Year by year the forest yielded to their sturdy blows. Each autumn new lands were laden with the harvest fruit. Orchards were planted, roads opened, new homes created. Before the expiration of the twenty years Nurse had conveyed to his children, their farms lying in every direction about him within the estate, a value having been made more than equal to the sum due to Allen. The homestead, with its immediate improvements, was retained by the patriarchal couple. Nurse's bond, which he had at the beginning given for a full deed, was canceled, and all was secured within his family. They had dared great things and succeeded. We shall meet them all in other and sadder relations.

Giles Corey was unlike any of the preceding characters. He was a man of much force, of great eccentricity, and of a peculiar tact in making enemies without really wronging any man. He was a man of sufficient wealth, though lacking all other qualifications, to occupy a first-class social position, to which, however, he seemed not to aspire.

He had lived for many years in the town of Salem, but for the last thirty years of his life had a homestead and farm in the "Middle Precinct," about two miles south-west of the village.

Corey's rough, heedless way of living made him the pack-horse for the sins committed in his neighborhood. At one time he whipped a man employed on his farm. The man was soon after carried by Corey's wife home to his friends sick, where subsequently he was, for some misconduct, whipped again. He soon after died. Much gossip grew out of this, and Corey was accused of killing the man. The complaint was not that he had whipped the man, for whipping by parents, guardians, and employers was "an institution" of those days, but that he had whipped him unmercifully. But nothing serious was proved against Corey, though the accusation was remembered.

At another time Corey's hired man, Gloyd, sued him for wages. The case, by mutual agreement, was left to impartial men. The decision was rather against Corey, but the referees say: "Giles Corey did manifest as much satisfaction, and gave as many thanks to every one of us as ever we heard." John Proctor, a neighbor, and the arbiter chosen by Gloyd, received, they add, "as many thanks from Corey as any one of those deciding the case." Proctor was a man of whom we shall know more—a blunt, sharp-cornered man, with some of Corey's roughness, but none of his doubtful morality. The two were enough alike to have passages at arms together in which the game was generally "a drawn" one. Soon after these kind words from Corey, Proctor's house caught fire. As there was seldom an evil abroad and Corey not thought to be the doer of it, the fire was attributed to him, Proctor joining in the accusation. Corey was brought to trial, and having proved that he was at home in bed when the fire was set, he was fully acquitted in law and in the judgment of all the candid. The accusations had been heaped upon him too heavily and too often, and the old man's spirit was up. He sued Proctor and others for defamation, and recovered damages against them all. But the law does not give character, and the accusations went on against Corey *to the bitter end*, though, at eighty years of age, he professed religion and was received into the First Church in Salem. Even the act of reception into the Church was most unjustly, and distastefully, as it seems to us, made the occasion for dishonoring his name. The Church Records read, to this day, against the entry of his name as a member, "a man eighty years old and *of a scandalous life*." God "blots out" our forgiven sins. Nothing more serious than an aptitude for making enemies seems to have been proved against this most notable man of the witchcraft history.

Giles Corey's wife, Martha, fills a noticeable place in the tragic scenes of our narrative. She was a member of the village Church, a praying, intelligent, clear-headed, resolute woman, worthy of a prominent place among the honored Puritan mothers of "the olden time." Her words and deeds and sufferings will become familiar to the reader.

George Jacobs, Sen., is presented to us as "an old man with two crutches." He had lived on his farm, about a mile and three fourths from the village and the same distance from the town, for fifty years, was of general good repute, and an honest tiller of the ground. His son, George Jacobs, Jun., a worthy son, will be remembered in connection with his own daughter Margaret, as well as with his venerable parent—a notable family.

The next portrait is a subject for study. It is that of a woman, but not that of a Puritan matron of the period of the witchcraft proceedings, though one of its prominent figures. She wears "a black cap and black hat, and a red paragon bodice, bordered and looped with different colors." Her conduct is as much out of the Puritanic order as her dress. Keeping a house for the entertainment of travelers, she keeps a "shovel-board" for their entertainment. The moral character of the play at shovel-board seems to have been much the same as that of our modern ten-pins or billiards. Her name is *Bridget Bishop.* She was the Widow Oliver before she was married to Bishop. Her husband is known as "The Sawyer," to distinguish him from several others of the same name. His business as a "sawyer" was not that of sawing wood for the fire, but that of sawing logs with the "pitsaw" into planks, joists, and framing lumber, for mechanical purposes.

Bridget was gifted in the same direction of Giles

Corey—she was wonderfully apt in making matter for gossip and in giving offense. She was brought to trial, under the accusation of witchcraft, twelve years before the great outbreak on that subject in Salem Village, and acquitted. It was a premature experiment upon the credulity of court and jury in Essex County. She, after this, defied public opinion, by her dress and conduct, more freely than ever. Slander was flippant at a distance, but found it not always safe to play its part in Bridget's presence, for she had a strong arm and resolute spirit. A man once boasted in the family of one of her neighbors that he would visit Bridget and "bring her out" as the bewitcher of their child. Accompanied by a boy, he tried the experiment. The offended woman penetrated his design, seized a spade, and, with lusty blows, drove both, bruised and crest-fallen, from her premises. Such conduct was not likely to advance Bridget's reputation for piety, she being a member of the Church in Beverly. Yet an investigation of the facts in her case, by her pastor, five years before the great witchcraft storm, resulted in showing that she was quite as much sinned against as sinning, and not, when treated fairly, otherwise than odd and imprudent.

Such are the portraits of some of those who will appear amid the scenes to be exhibited.

CHAPTER III.

The Beginning of Strife.

WE have glanced at the locality in which the scenes of our narrative are laid. We have briefly introduced the representative persons, noticing most fully those who are to become actors in the tragedies of our story or victims of its bloody progress. There were contentions between certain parties spread over the few years immediately preceding the trials and executions, some of which were intensely bitter, protracted, and ultimately, wide-spread. These are believed, by many careful students of the witchcraft history, to have been the occasion of some of its worst features, and to account largely for its very existence.

As is generally the case, this story of strife is a long one; but what might and has, no doubt, occupied a whole winter of evening fireside talk we must narrate in a short chapter.

The General Court had, in 1632, granted Governor Endicott three hundred acres of land. The grant was located in the north-east corner of Salem town, not far from the Beverly line. It was described in the records as being "bounded on the south side with a river commonly called the Cow

House River; on the north side with a river commonly called the Duck River; on the east with a river, leading up to the two former rivers, known by the name of Wooleston River; and on the west with the main-land."

This made, throwing out, as was usual, the unavailable swamps, the required three hundred acres. In 1636 the town, which now disposed of its lands, gave Townsend Bishop a grant on the west of Endicott's of three hundred acres. It was loosely described in the conveyance, fixing the number of rods in each direction, but not determining with exactness where they should begin and end.

At a later period Endicott bought the Townsend Bishop land. When his oldest son, John Endicott, Jr., was married, the Governor gave him the Townsend Bishop Farm. The papers which were intended to make this legal were, unfortunately, not such as to leave no room for an honest difference of opinion concerning their meaning. The father died in 1665. After a protracted lawsuit between John and his brother Zerubbabel, the Court, which had vacillated in the course of the trials, established John in possession of the Bishop estate. John died in February, 1668, without children, and left his whole property to his wife, who, six months after, married Rev. James Allen, one of the ministers of the First Church in Boston, whose former wife had left him a large property. His Endicott wife died in April, 1673, leaving him all her property, and in September of the same year he married again. The surviving members of the Endicott family thus saw in a few years a fair portion of the paternal estate swept into the hands of strangers in the most distasteful and provoking manner. But this was but the beginning of their trouble.

In April, 1678, Allen sold the Bishop estate to Francis Nurse. We have sketched the history of Nurse, the terms on which he bought the farm, the skillful and energetic way in which he, his sons, and sons-in-law wrought out those terms, planting, as their families increased, new farms on their ample acres, heroically penetrating the wooded depths with cultivated fields, thus holding in fruitful cultivation every foot which they conquered from the wilderness. Through many of the years in which the Nurses were thus toiling a most painful lawsuit was going on in the courts, involving the money, mind, and heart of distinguished parties concerning these very acres. Zerubbabel Endicott, who lived on the original portion of the paternal estate, which became known as the Orchard Farm, had never acknowledged the equity of the decision of the Court in favor of his brother John, which gave to "his heirs and assigns" the Bishop Farm. His feelings, then, may be imagined when he found his Orchard Farm itself, including the vicinity of the homestead, assailed by persistent, greedy, and reckless claimants. The facts are these: Lands, at later times, had been granted to various parties on the north, south, and west of the Bishop Farm, now owned by the Nurses. Allen had guaranteed to Francis Nurse, according to the terms originally given to Bishop, three hundred acres. But owners on every side had so fixed their boundaries on alleged rights from the courts, that this number of acres could not be included within its limits without pushing over the claims of some one or more of the neighbors. Each stood defiantly upon his own border, and all others agreed, as it seems, to combine against Endicott, push the Bishop Farm into the Orchard Farm until the required acres were obtained. This they did, and, after long protracted contests from court to court. they triumphed over Endicott, bringing the boundary line of the strangers over the paternal lands within sight of his door. His health and his heart were broken. Allen, who was rich, standing among the foremost of the metropolitan ministers, and in the midst of court friends, fought the battle in the interest of the Nurses, as he had stipulated. Nathaniel Putnam (let his name be noted in this connection) was his chief coadjutor. Putnam owned lands bordering on the north-east corner of the Bishop Farm, and owned also lands on its south-west side. He possessed skill in management, and will in execution. Such a fight gave him a congenial inspiration. Endicott at one time sent teams and men into a part of the disputed territory claimed by Putnam to fell trees and hew them into the frame of a house. One morning, going to their work, they found neither timber nor frame. Putnam had sent men and teams, cleaned them all out, and piled them up near his house. Endicott sued him and lost his case. Oppression seems to have made Endicott mad, though generally amiable, wise, and just. The Nurse family took no part in the legal process of the strife, but, being in possession, they held themselves ready to repel aggressions. Endicott, after the case had been finally decided against him, was unwise enough to send his men into the wood-lot, lost in the contest, to cut fire-wood. When they had loaded their teams, Nurse's men came and pitched the wood off. This "battle of the wilderness" lasted two days. Once, at least, Nurse and Endicott were there in person, leading to the fight their respective forces, for it appears from the records that Nurse demanded of the aggressors whose men they were, when Endicott stepped forward, saying, "They are my men!"

Whether the woody and wordy strife ended in blows we know not; but it ended in a lawsuit of course, in which Endicott was the loser.

We need not the testimony that appeared at the trials to assure us that the ultimate result of these disputes was a general and partisan animosity.

Our narrative next opens upon another occasion of strife which brings us nearer the main portion of our history. It was that which grew out of the establishment of Salem Village as a separate parish. The farmers of that part of the town lying mainly north petitioned in 1670 for the privilege of providing a house of worship and minister for themselves. The reasons for this were amply found in their distance from the town; but jealousy of the town management of society affairs may have given its promptings. In 1672 the town consented, and the General Court gave its legal sanction. But several significant conditions were imposed. They were not to be exempt from taxes in support of the town Church until they had a house of worship and had raised a support for a minister of their own; and they were not to form a Church until a minister was ordained over them; and such ordination was not to take place without the consent of the mother Church. The latter portion of these terms was as hard for the one party faithfully to perform, as it was inconsistent for the other to impose. As we shall see, it engendered strife.

The parish thus commencing its separate career was the Salem Village, the locality of the origin and general center of the witchcraft movements.

Besides the fire in the rear from the mother Church, the Village had a "border war."

Between the Village and Ipswich River on the north there was a neutral ground, understood not to belong to any town by the terms of their grants made prior to 1639. At that time the Court gave it to Salem, and on its faith Salem Village people pushed their clearings into it, and dotted it in a few years with their homes. Some years later the General Court, with a careless disregard of their own previous action, so apparent in the Bishop and Orchard Farm quarrel, authorized other parties to settle there independent of the Salem jurisdiction. Still later, the General Court created the town of Topsfield, and included the greater part of these lands within its borders. Salem raised its voice against this, but was not heard. The Village protested and were disregarded. The settlers on the disputed territory, who were thus transferred from Salem, without their consent, to the outskirts of the new town, held their homes in sullen defiance. Topsfield levied rates upon them and payment was refused. Constables and tax collectors were sent to them in vain. The matter went into the courts, and, what was worse, into local man-to-man contests.

John Putnam had gone to these lands, and he and his sons had built houses, cultivated fields, and planted orchards. One day Jacob Town and John How, "Topsfield men," came within his claim and cut down trees. Putnam hearing the chopping went out and remonstrated; but as they defied him and were two to one, he had to brook the insult. Soon after he took a force of sons and nephews to the spot, and they took their turn at chopping. The sound of the axes brought on the Topsfield men—Isaac Easty, Sen., John Easty, Joseph Town, Jun.—who came to put a stop to the proceedings. On reaching the spot they warned Putnam off. He replied, "The timber now and here cut down has been felled by me and my orders; and I will keep cutting and carrying away from this land until next March."

"What! by violence?" interposed the Topsfield men.

"Ay, by violence!" answered Putnam. "You

may sue me. You know where I dwell;" and, turning to his men, he said, "Fall on." The Topsfield men, being the weaker party this time, beat a retreat, doubtless to recruit and renew the attack.

We shall meet again the actors in this incident.

This border warfare had been going on for a whole generation, widening and intensifying with every collision, when the witchcraft delusion broke out.

We turn to relative and nearer views of that great event.

CHAPTER IV.

The Flock and the Shepherds.

THE farmers of Salem Village having obtained the privilege, as we have stated, of building a church and employing a minister for themselves, acted promptly in the matter. A parsonage house was built, "forty-two feet in length, twenty feet broad, thirteen feet stud, four chimneys, and no gable ends." A "lean-to" was added at a later time. It was located in the center of the Village, and a generous parishioner gave for the use of the Pastor five and a half acres of land. An acre of land was given near it for the house of worship, and one was erected, thirty-four feet by twenty-eight, and "sixteen feet between joints." Two end galleries and a pulpit canopy were added. The town Church having just finished a new meeting-house gave the villagers their old pulpit and deacon's seat, which were, no doubt with fitting acknowledgments, received and duly assigned their places.

Thus were these sanctuaries made ready for holy purposes, doubtless with devout prayer by many that the Divine Presence might fill them. It was well, perhaps, that such could not see "the giving over to Satan" which should precede his coming. They might have been faint and weary in their minds during the painful waiting.

The Rev. James Bayley, a native of Newbury, came from that town in 1671 and united with the Church in Salem. He was a graduate of Harvard College in the class of 1669, and a man of talents, culture, and Christian spirit. He was employed to preach in the Village. An evil spirit, not from the Lord, we think, awaited his coming in the hearts of a portion of the people. Whether it was that strife had become a seated distemper, or from some fancied irregularity in his reception into the Salem Church and his coming among them, is not clear. As they did not heed the divine counsel to "leave off strife before it be meddled with," it became to them like the letting out of water. He was employed from year to year, amid heated discussions and bitter altercations, which, like the breath of a pestilence, scattered poison far and wide—in this case a deadly moral poison. It reached so destructive a crisis in 1679 that both parties applied to the mother Church for conciliatory intervention. It was granted and failed.

The General Court was next appealed to, and at first it uttered its mandate to the villagers, in behalf of the minister and his friends, with withering severity, but toned down, in conclusion, to timid advice; the consequence was that it was as little heeded as the mother Church, and the consuming fire burned the brighter for these stirrings. At this point Mr. Bayley wisely withdrew from the uncomfortable position. More than three to one of the parish were numbered among his friends; but his enemies were men of power, among whom was Nathaniel Putnam of the Endicott fight. He was, however, a generous though a conquering foe. He joined with others in a parting gift to Mr. Bayley of "twenty-eight acres of upland, and thirteen of meadow in all."

During these years of quarrel it will be recollected that Salem Village had no organized Church, as they could not agree among themselves, nor, consequently, secure the approbation of the town Church in the ordination of a minister. The General Court, by a special act, had authorized "the householders" to do the parish business without any reference to their being, or not being, professors of religion, and ordered them to choose two men to collect the rates and pay the Pastor—to be, in fact, Deacons without a Church.

Mr. Bayley during his stay at the Village had, in addition to his parish troubles, great domestic sorrow. His wife and three children had died. This, it will be seen, as well as the former, came into sad significance when the troubles of Salem Village came to their terrific consummation. His wife was Mary Carr, from Salisbury. Her sister Ann, when only a child of not quite sixteen, had married Sergeant Thomas Putnam, clerk of the parish, nephew of Nathaniel, being the oldest son of his elder brother. Sergeant Thomas had already shown his fighting qualities in a campaign against the Narragansett Indians. Of course, he and his family were partisans of Mr. Bayley.

At a little later period, and quite near the witchcraft outbreak, Sergeant Thomas and his brother added to their complicity with the border and parish strife a quarrel, all their own, over the will of their deceased father.

In 1680 Salem Village invited to their pulpit Rev. George Burroughs. He graduated at Harvard College in 1670, and had preached at Casco, (now Portland,) Maine, where he had won much favor by his self-sacrificing spirit in the common dangers and hardships of a new country, as well as by his faithful and able performance of the immediate duty of a minister. He came poor to his new flock, and special appropriations were made to establish his family in the parsonage. But the friends of Mr. Bayley were now the assailants of the Pastor. Old animosities were revived with a new victim. The parish business was neglected and the minister unpaid. At the close of his first year his wife died, and he had to contract a debt for her decent interment. No wonder that he was disgusted, and soon after, abandoning both his claims and his sheep, many of whom seemed more like wolves, removed from the Village. In 1683 the parish turned for relief to the Court, stating their shepherdless condition, and requesting that honorable body to command Mr. Burroughs to come to the Village for a mutual investigation of accounts. This the Court did, and the Pastor immediately obeyed the summons.

On his arrival the householders were called together, and for several days a quiet, orderly settlement was progressing. On the afternoon of the third day, when all was approaching a peaceful conclusion, and an opening was seen in the angry clouds which had darkened the assembly, it suddenly closed, and a storm burst upon the people. John Putnam, as chairman of the parish Society, had agreed with Burroughs to accept an order on the Society, which was yet largely in debt to its Pastor, in payment of a personal demand. Matters thus stood when the Marshal came in and whispered to Putnam. Putnam answers: "You know what you have to do; do your office." The Marshal turns to Burroughs and attaches his body for Putnam's adjusted claim. Burroughs replies: "I have no goods to show; I am now reckoning with the inhabitants, for we know not yet who is in debt; but here is my body," and after a pause adds, "What will you do with me?"

The Marshal seemed reluctant to do the shameful business, turned to Putnam and said, "What shall I do?" Putnam, after conferring with his brother Thomas, answered, "Marshal, take your prisoner and have him to the ordinary, and secure him till morning." The "ordinary" was the public-house used as a lock-up. In the course of this proceeding on the part of Putnam, Deacon Ingersall, the intimate friend of the Putnams, but a just and brave man for the right, arose in the meeting and, addressing John Putnam, said, "Lieutenant, I wonder you attach Mr. Burroughs for the money when, to my knowledge, you and Mr. Burroughs have reckoned and balanced accounts two or three times since, as you say, it was due; and you never made any mention of it when you reckoned with Mr. Burroughs."

John Putnam answered, "It is true, and I own it."

Nathaniel Ingersall and others then interposed, became security for Burroughs's debt to Putnam, and saved him from imprisonment. The friendly settlement was brought thus suddenly to a close, and Burroughs again left the Village.

Our adieus to the good man are mingled with sadness for his wrongs. When, under still more painful circumstances, we bestow upon him our farewell blessings, it will be in sadder and deeper tones.

The people of Salem Village were not dependent upon the presence of the Pastor for a first-class quarrel, though they had found such a presence convenient for that object. Their parish records had been badly kept. Decisions had been entered in them which, it was alleged, had never been voted, and important votes had not been recorded. Many meetings were called on the matter, and stormy sessions were held. Then, as a reserve force, lest the fighting zeal should flag, some one ascertained, or thought he did, that the title to their ministry lands was not good—that somebody was to blame about it, and ought to set the business right. Disputes were thrown in about the use of lands around the meeting-house. No wonder, then, that when, in 1684, the Rev. Deodat Lawson commenced his ministry among them he had shown a reluctance to respond to their call. He was a man of learning, ability, and, as we shall have occasion to know, of pulpit power. For awhile, at least, these other materials for strife left the Pastor in comparative peace. But when, in 1686, they submitted the question of his ordination to a parish meeting, they did not give the required vote.

Failing to come to terms on disputed questions, in 1687, at a legal meeting, the householders put the debated questions into the hands of a large committee, with Lieutenant, now "Captain" John Putnam as chairman, for settlement, wisely adding that if they could not agree they should submit them to the reverend Elders of the town, in connection with Major Gedney and John Hathorne, Esqs.

Of course the Village committee did not agree, and the above gentlemen, with William Brown, Jr., Esq., added, took up the matter.

Their report goes straight to the mark. They tell the Villagers that the steps toward the ordination of Mr. Lawson had not been altogether "inoffensively" managed; that the hinderances to it were not of sufficient weight to be decisive; that their "uncomely reflections, tossed to and fro," would, if not timely prevented, "let out peace and order, and let in confusion and every evil work." After appending some suggestions about their records, and that their spirits "should be better quieted and composed" before proceeding to ordination, they close the report by curtly remarking, "But if our advice be rejected we wish you better, and hearts to follow it; and only add, if you will unreasonably trouble yourselves, we pray you not any further to trouble us."

The Villagers called a meeting, heard the report, and voted to "accept of and embrace" its advice, but added, "in general, not in parts;" which meant, we suppose, that they would accept such of it as they liked—that is, walk by their *own* counsels as heretofore. They did succeed, in some measure, in righting their records, but not in voting to ordain Mr. Lawson; and he, not seeing a prospect of their minds being sufficiently composed for that purpose, left them. While Mr. Lawson was preaching at the Village he lost his wife and daughter. It is singular that domestic as well as parish troubles should have attended each of their pastors.

If the flock up to this period had annoyed the shepherds, they were now to reap as they had sown, and take their turn in being annoyed. Rev. Thomas Parris was invited, with a unity of action and feeling unusual with the Village, to be their minister. He played shy, begged time to consider so weighty a matter, wearied the fathers of the parish in his protracted negotiations, drew out "the younger men," made with them sharp terms of compensation, engaged himself to them early in 1689, and was ordained the latter part of the same year. Thus the Village had, at last, a Church.

The rainbow of peace, at Mr. Parris's coming, was dimly seen through the parting clouds which had so long discharged upon Salem Village its devastating storms. But it soon closed, and the heavens grew blacker, threatening still severer tempests.

In the bargain which the Pastor had made with "Young America" he had received at least encouragement that the parsonage and the ministry lands should be conveyed to him and his heirs in their sole and perpetual right. This feature of the contract leaked out and raised a storm. Yet *somehow*, nobody knew how, a record found its way to the parish books covering such agreement which the parish had never made. There were excited gatherings to consider the matter; fierce words were uttered; old animosities were revived with intensified elements; parties re-arranged themselves defiantly face to face, and the Church, dedicated to the God of peace, began to have an earnest of the scenes which soon awaited it.

Some of the most skillful managers and persistent workers were banded against Mr. Parris. He had a Church for awhile subservient to him, and he played the Church against the parish, and, in his extremity, through them invoked the court against his opposers. He threw around his religious services, especially his Church meetings, an awe-inspiring solemnity which he was accused of using to carry selfish, worldly ends, and to crush his enemies. In the former quarrels it was an exacting parish against yielding ministers. Now parish and minister were well matched, and the fight was a grand one to all the enemies of religion.

We shall leave Mr. Parris for awhile on the eve of being crushed by the leading spirits of the opposition. When next we meet him we shall find him master of the situation, with a skillfully changed mode of attack and new weapons.

CHAPTER V.

A Sad, Universal Delusion.

WE have seen how the people of Salem Village sowed the wind. Before giving the details of the whirlwind which they reaped, we pause to show that they were not sinners above all their generation because they suffered such things; and that their credulity as to certain Satanic influences, which served to conduct the lightning of the storm down upon their devoted heads, was not peculiar to them, but was common to their own and many preceding ages, and included all classes of the people.

The term witchcraft had obtained a peculiar meaning. Those accepting and using it believed that the devil entered into a specific covenant with certain persons, and, through them, and in accordance with the terms of this covenant, he wrought great evil in the Church of Christ, torturing the bodies and destroying the souls of men. They held that much of his power to oppose the kingdom of grace in the world was wholly dependent upon this voluntary human agency. He came in various forms to those whom he would make agents, generally as "the black man," but often in the shape or "apparition" of those already in league with him. A book was presented and a formal bargain proposed. Of course, the seducer being master of all the arts of deception, the terms were varied to suit the character and moral condition of the victim. The deceiver promised on his part to make his confederates rich, eloquent, gifted in the fine arts, great in physical strength, according to the terms of the specific bargain. He conferred upon them truly wonderful powers, according to this strange belief. They could raise a storm at sea which should baffle the skill of the most experienced seaman and overcome the resistance of the strongest ships, sweep over the land with a tornado, rend forests, unroof houses, and, as was their special delight, demolish the churches. Fire and plague did their bidding. They could pinch, throttle, burn, set on and crush those whom they wished to afflict; and, more than this, deprive them of reason, and take their lives. They could blight the fruits of the earth and send poverty and desolation through a whole community. In all this they delighted. Having transferred their allegiance from God to the devil, they ruled with him in this lower world. They were not, of course, obliged to be present in person where they wrought this evil. They could go in their "shape" or "apparition," or send their representative in the form of some animal, as a dog, black cat, hog, toad, mouse, or rat. "A yellow-bird" figures prominently in this mythology, and we shall have an opportunity to become quite well acquainted with it. These witch kings and queens had their courtiers to do their bidding, and in such a courtly form as well befitted them. A spider commonly represented them, and sad it was for a poor accused person, when cast into a dusty, unswept, and unused cell, if the keeper found near her person a spider which he failed to capture.

The witches had conferred upon them an extensive range of knowledge, yet they seem not to have anticipated any of the modern methods of travel, but continued, from one generation to another, in the same old witch way of passing through the air on a stick; and, as we learn from sundry witnesses under oath in court, they often took their new recruits behind them.

Shakspeare expresses the belief of his day in the power of witches in the following eloquent language:

> I conjure you by that which you profess,
> Howe'er you come to know it, answer me;
> Though you undo the winds and let them fight
> Against the churches; though the yeasty waves
> Confound and swallow navigation up;
> Though bladed corn be lodged, and trees blown down;
> Though castles topple on their warder's head;
> Though palaces and pyramids do slope
> Their heads to their foundations; though the treasures
> Of nature's genius tumble all together,
> Even till destruction sicken; answer me
> To what I answer you.—*Macbeth.*

Witch science taught that the devil set his mark upon the bodies of his confederates, and that the place marked became callous and dead, losing utterly its sensibility, so that it might be pricked or cut without producing pain. These marks sometimes assumed the form of teats, from which the imps received their nourishment.

This science also taught that witches made representatives of persons they wished to torment, called puppets: a doll, the figure of animals, or even a roll of rags, were used as such representatives. When these were pinched, pricked, cuffed, or crushed, the like happened to the victims selected. An eminent minister of Boston, a great and good man, whom we shall meet in the course of our story, expresses an opinion that the witches sometimes used their own bodies as puppets, pinching and pricking themselves, for instance, that others might be pricked and pinched; but we are incredulous as to such an unselfish practice of witches, unless indeed it was in some extreme case, when they were hard pressed for the means of tormenting.

We need not say how utterly unsupported by Scripture, reason, or facts this whole witchcraft theory was. But law-makers believed it, and conformed their legislation to their faith. If a person was accused of being a witch, and of having tortured, or even murdered, a specified individual, it was in vain that he proved that he was in another place, even a thousand miles away, at the time of the murder. The law recognized his capability of committing the act in apparition or by an imp.

Provisions were made by legislation for a search by a jury of the same sex, a surgeon being present, of all parts of the body of an accused person. Any callous or unusual marks, such as aged persons or persons who had been subjects of special bodily inflictions were liable to have, were easily sworn to by excited, credulous people, as witch-marks.

It was believed that the devil sought shining marks in those with whom he sought to make covenants, and that aged and prominent Church members of life-long, unsullied reputation were especially desired. We can readily credit so much as to our arch Accuser's *desire*, but the light consideration which witchcraft believers put upon long years of undoubted piety, when weighed against specter accusations, was very sad, as we shall have occasion to feel.

Not only law-makers, but the highest courts throughout the world, gave their sanction to witchcraft. Sir Matthew Hale, the great and good judge of England in the middle of the seventeenth century, threw his influence in its favor. The execution of two females, in 1664, who were tried before him and received the death sentence from his lips, gave the sanction of his great name to the delusion, and was used in vindication of their conduct by the American judges at Salem.

The seventeenth century may be termed the great witchcraft century. In it many books were written in its favor by some great and good men, as well as by many weak and foolish ones. King James of England, a pretentious but weak ruler, wrote in its support, and the Parliament, to flatter him, echoed his opinions in bloody laws. Perhaps it was by the same influence that the words "witch" and "witchcraft" were introduced in our present version of the Scriptures, which was made in his reign, thus seeming to give the sanction of the Bible to assumptions concerning demonology which it nowhere teaches.

The physicians every-where shouted "*vive la* witchcraft." It was a godsend to them, for when they had in charge a patient whose case baffled their skill it was a convenient resort to insinuate that "an evil hand" was upon him, or plainly to refer the trouble to witch inflictions.

Thus established in the popular faith and enthroned in high places, witchcraft for many generations swept over the nations like the angel of death. In the year 1515 five hundred were burned in Geneva in three months. "Almost an infinite number," says one writer, "were burned for witchcraft in France"—a thousand in a single diocese. A modern German writer on witchcraft history says that in Bamberg alone, between 1624 and 1630, there were seven hundred and eighty-five processes against witches. In England and Scotland the executions were numerous, attended by the most painful details, and quite as devoid of reason and humanity as those occurring in Salem.

The spirit with which the witchcraft prosecutions were carried on in England is well-illustrated by the following incident.

A man by the name of Matthew Hopkins, shrewdly taking advantage of the public infatuation, made witch detection a profession. He styled himself a "Witch-finder General." He traveled over the country under the sanction of the government, fastening suspicion upon whomsoever he pleased, having his expenses paid from the public treasury, and drawing a fee for each person convicted, thus being stimulated by a bribe to make the number as large as his love of gain might be greedy. In one year, in one county alone, three-score died under his hand. He was armed with the power to torture, which he used in a manner to entitle him to an official position in a papal inquisition. A venerable clergyman of the Church of England was hanged through the application of his detective policy.

But the English race on either continent have never shown that it was safe, for any great length of time, to presume upon their credulity as a basis of oppression. Hopkins had adopted, among other absurd methods of detecting witches, this one: He tied the thumb of the right hand to the great toe of the left foot, thus doubling his victim into a painful position; a rope was then tied to him and he was dragged through a river or pond. If he floated, he was condemned as a witch. Having practiced this outrage a little too long, some gentlemen applied the test to himself, tied his thumb and toe together, and dragged him through a pond. He floated, and stood condemned by his own test. If he had not floated it is likely he would have been drowned, which would have been a befitting end for the wretch. As it was, his official career as *Witch-finder General* thus ingloriously closed.

We turn to glance at the relation of the American colonies to this universal delusion at the time when the darkening clouds were gathering over Salem Village.

CHAPTER VI.

Strange Things.

IT could not be supposed that so prevalent a belief as that we have described in the last chapter would be rejected by the early settlers of America, surrounded as they had been by it in the Old World.

Even the thoughtful and devout Penn presided at a witchcraft trial, and failed, it is said, to secure the execution of the accused only by an informality in the indictment.

Margaret Jones of Charlestown was hanged in Boston in 1648, after a trial for witchcraft in which all the frivolous circumstances were allowed in evidence which so disgraced the Salem courts. In 1656 a Mrs. Hibbins, a sister of the then acting lieutenant-governor, a widow of a man of wealth, and an excellent, sensible woman, was hanged in Boston for witchcraft, the General Court itself condemning her, and designating lecture-day, "presently after the lecture," as the time.

Hartford, Springfield, and other places, had visitations of the pestilential disease. But we leave the details of these to notice certain very strange occurrences, quite near enough to Salem Village for it to feel their full influence. These were used, it will be seen, as occasions for accusations of witchcraft, and they did quicken and deepen the belief in its reality. Yet they may be considered, we think, entirely aside from that belief, and wholly on their own merits. We refer to strange acting of children in various places, to noises which could not be accounted for, and seeming life given to material things which rattled loosely about the house. We give a few examples.

The following is an extract from a detailed account of Elizabeth Knapp, of Groton, by her Pastor, the Rev. Samuel Willard. It is contained in "The Mather Papers." Mr. Willard was afterward minister of the Old South Church in Boston, and was creditably connected with the witchcraft of 1692.

"This poor and miserable object, about a fortnight before she was taken, we observed to carry herself in a strange and unwonted manner. Sometimes she would give sudden shrieks, and if we inquired a reason, would always put us off with some excuse, and then would burst forth into immoderate and extravagant laughter, in such a wise as sometimes she fell on to the ground with it. I myself observed oftentimes a strange change in her countenance, and could not suspect the true reason, but conceived she might be ill, and divers times inquired how she did, and she always answered, 'Well;' which made me wonder. But the tragedy began to unfold itself about Monday, October 30, 1671, on this manner, (as I received by credible information, being that day myself gone from home.) In the evening, a little before she went to bed, sitting by the fire, she cried out, 'O, my legs!' and clapt her hands on them; immediately, 'O, my heart!' and removed her hand thither; and forthwith, 'O, I am strangled!' and put her hands on her throat. Those who observed her could not see what to make of it, whether she was in earnest or dissembled, and in this manner they left her complaining her breath was stopt. Next day she was in a strange frame, as was observed by divers persons, sometimes weeping, sometimes laughing, and making many apish gestures. In the evening going into the cellar she shrieked suddenly, and being inquired as to the cause, she answered that she saw two persons in the cellar; whereupon some went down with her to search, but found none, she also looking with them. At last she turned her head, and looking one way steadily, used the expression, 'What cheer, old man?' which they that were with her took for a fancy and so ceased. Afterwards, the same evening, the rest of the family being in bed, she was, as one lying in the room saw, and she herself afterward related, suddenly thrown down into the midst of the floor with violence, and taken with a violent fit, whereupon the whole family was raised, and with much ado was she kept out of the fire from destroying herself. After which time she was followed by fits from thence till the Sabbath-day, in which she was violent in bodily motions, leapings, strainings, and strange agitations, scarce to be held in bounds by the strength of three or four;

violent also in roarings and screamings, representing a dark resemblance of hellish torments, and frequently using in these fits divers words, sometimes crying out 'Money, money!' sometimes, 'Sin and misery!' with other words."

The physician was wisely called, who, thinking that her trouble might be, in part at least, a bodily one, prescribed for her. The Christian friends resorted to earnest prayer. Her afflictions went on for several weeks. She for awhile denied any covenant with the devil, though she claimed that he had appeared to her for several years and in various forms, urging her "to sign the book." Later she indulged in many contradictions about the matter, but finally settled down in persistent denial. She also claimed to be bewitched, and named a worthy woman of the neighborhood as the tormentor. When the accused was brought into her presence she was terribly tortured, even, as it was alleged, before she knew of her presence. But Mr. Willard was cautious in receiving such evidence against one otherwise known to be good, though the girl affirmed that her apparition in a riding-hood had come down the chimney to her that night. But the Pastor watched and cross-questioned her, and, detecting her in some twistings, refused her credit against the accused. The result was that the girl ceased impeaching. This will be remembered to the minister's credit when we come to contrast his management with that of the courts at the Salem trials.

Her acting at last took a new turn. She crowed

like a cock and barked like a dog. This was improved by a voice speaking within her—"a grum, low, yet audible voice it was." It was the Sabbath when this commenced, and it railed against the girl's parents for "going to hear a black rogue who told them nothing but a parcel of lies." When Mr. Willard came in the voice called out, "O, you are a great rogue!" He called for a light, sat down and watched her organs of speech while the voice heaped abuse upon him, and he declares that he could detect no motion, not even of the lips, when the letters b, m, and p, were in frequent use.

Mr. Willard does not strongly affirm the supernatural source of all this strange acting, but plainly leans to the opinion that it was diabolical.

Governor Hutchinson, referring to this case in his history, though he gives no details, calls the girl "a ventriloqua." The reader is at liberty to adopt the opinion of either the governor or minister.

The story of the Goodwin children, whose acting occurred in 1688, as related by Cotton Mather, is well known, and we need give only an item or two of its long story.

There were four children affected by the peculiar inspiration, the oldest being only about thirteen years old. Barking and mewing were parts of their accomplishments, to which they added flying. "Yea, they would fly like geese, and be carried with incredible swiftness, having but just their toes now and then upon the ground, sometimes not once in twenty feet, and their arms waved like the wings of a bird."

One of the children had less pleasant exercises. She was roasted, she said, in an oven, and the perspiration, at the same time, streamed from her face. Suddenly she received a dash of cold water, and she shivered and quaked under the violent transition. She bounded about the rooms and up the stairs on the back of an invisible horse, which came unbidden to her service.

Mr. Mather kindly took her to his house to try the effects of religious influence upon her, especially that of prayer in her behalf, and, we presume, to detect, if possible, any trick or dissembling. His qualifications for the latter service were, it must be conceded, much less than those of Mr. Willard.

Among the girl's wonderful doings in Mr. Mather's home was, not her *speaking* unknown tongues, but her understanding them. The minister was a young man of wonderful attainments, and, one day, not wishing the girl to know what he said to a third person, he talked in Latin. She looked knowingly, and he believed she understood him; he then continued the conversation in Greek; she had the same understanding of what he said. Amazed, he talked away in Hebrew, but she at once, and with the same ease, apprehended it. Even a Doctor of Divinity in these days would have been cornered by this time, but not so Mr. Mather, who, although not at this time a D. D., could converse in seven languages; hence, nothing daunted, he rattled on in the Iroquois language. The girl, or, as Mr. Mather inferred, the evil spirit which possessed her, not understanding Iroquois, was defeated in this strife of tongues.

But a stranger case occurred in Newbury, commencing in 1679, which, as it was nearer Salem Village, must have exerted a more decided influence upon it than any other. We shall give it more in detail, and if the reader observes closely all the circumstances he will be able to form his own opinion of their character. The study of such facts is necessary to a just and thorough understanding of the witchcraft history.

William Morse's house was strangely assailed. An old sailor by the name of Caleb Powell, happening to be on shore, went, with an incredulous mind, to see the "tippings" and to hear the "rappings." Morse and his wife had living with them a grandson, a mere boy as it seems. Powell condoled with the old people in their fright, and charged the mischief upon the boy. He affirmed also that he knew something of the black-art, and that by astrology and astronomy he could find out whether there were diabolical transactions about the house of Morse, and he thought he should try. This brought the court down upon the sailor, and he was tried for witchcraft, but acquitted. During the trial the following testimony was rendered. We make selections, exhibiting fairly its character:

"The testimony of William Morse, which saith, together with his wife, aged about sixty-five years, that, Thursday night, being the twenty-seventh day of November, we heard a great noise without, round the house, of knocking the boards of the house, and, as we conceived, throwing of stones against the house. Whereupon myself and wife looked out and saw nobody, and the boy all this time with us; but we had stones and sticks thrown at us that we were forced to retire into the house again. Afterward we went to bed, and the boy with us; and then the noise was upon the roof of the house. . . . The next morning a stick of links hanging in the chimney, they were thrown out of their place, and we hanged them up again, and they were thrown down again and some into the fire. . . .

"The next day being Saturday, stones, sticks, and pieces of brick came down, (the chimney,) so that we could not quietly cook our breakfast; and sticks of fire also came down at the same time.

"The next day, being the Sabbath, many stones and sticks and pieces of bricks came down the chimney. On Monday, Mr. Richardson and my brother being there, the frame of my cow house they saw very firm. I sent my boy out to scare the fowls from my hog's meat; he went to the cow house and it fell down, my boy crying with the hurt of the fall. In the afternoon, the pots hanging over the fire did dash so vehemently one against the other, we sat down one that they might not dash to pieces. I saw the andiron leap into the pot, and dance and leap out again, and leap on a table and there abide, and my wife saw the andiron on the table. Also I saw the pot turn itself over, and throw down all the water. Again we saw a tray with wool leap up and down, and throw the wool out, and so many times, and saw nobody meddle with it. Again a tub, his hoop fly off of itself and the tub turn over, and nobody near it. Again the woolen wheel turned upside down and stood up on its end and a spade sat on it. Stephen Greenleafe saw it, and myself and my wife. . . . Again, my wife and boy making the bed, the chest did open and shut; the bedclothes could not be made to lie on the bed, but fly off again."

The neighbors, of course, came in to see these wonders, some of whom give their testimony:

"John Dole saw a pine stick of candle-wood to fall down, a stove, and fire-brand; and these things he saw not what way they came, till they fell down by him.

"The same was observed by John Tucker; the boy was in one corner, whom they saw and observed all the while, and saw no motion in him."

Mr. Powell came in at this point in the affair, and, after considerable solicitation, was permitted to remove the boy from his grandparents, after which, as the grandfather testifies, they had entire quiet. It seems, however, that he returned, for the testimony shows a renewal of a great deal more of the strange proceedings, with the boy present. Anthony Morse, brother of William, testifies to being at his brother's house and seeing some of the most extraordinary of these actings. Powell testifies that, looking in the window at one time when Morse was at prayer, he saw the boy throw a shoe at the old man's head.

Powell was competent to testify to what he saw, but he did not come to Morse's house, as we understand the testimony to say, until after what we have above quoted transpired. How much of the above is "rose-colored" we cannot tell; but we must remember that it was given under oath, and is a testimony to a matter-of-fact, and not of mere opinion. If it be true that two persons saw "the andiron leap into the pot, and dance and leap out again, and leap on a table and there abide," it is plain that the boy could not have done so much, though he could throw a shoe at his grandfather's head while he was at prayer.

Those who assume that there was the presence here of evil, invisible spirits, easily dispose of the fact of the quiet in the boy's absence by the inference that it was a part of the diabolism to fix the responsibility upon some human agent, and thus precipitate witchcraft executions.

Failing to convict Powell, the authorities carried the poor old grandmother to Boston, where she was tried and sentenced to be hanged, but was pardoned by Governor Bradstreet against the popular clamor.

CHAPTER VII.

The Circle.

THE facts that we have narrated must have had their influence upon the people of Salem Village. Their disputes embittered their spirits. The occurrence of Satanic operations, as they believed, all about them, inflamed their feelings of resentment. They considered, in common with all the colonists, this land theirs, not only as to the encroachments of men opposed to their particular political and religious views, but as to these evident, malicious intents of the devil. They believed this new country to be a peculiarly advantageous field for the triumph of the Gospel; and the arch enemy, jealous of this fact, as they thought, seemed to be challenging them to a contest for this advantage, and they were not the men to receive such a defiant challenge tamely. Lieutenant Governor Danforth, on the strength of present manifestations, had begun to make arrests for witchcraft, and the prison doors had been closed on several suspected persons.

In addition to these already stated reasons for morbid excitement, early writers on this subject have suggested the recent death of some of the fathers, the departure now of nearly all of those whose counsels had been trusted, and whose leadership had been confidently followed. Besides, their political affairs were in a confused state. The King had taken away their charter, and they stood trembling before the incoming order of things, not knowing what evil should befall them. Within were fightings, and without were fears.

If there were to be severer contests either with visible or invisible powers, the people of Salem Village, as we have seen, were not made of the stuff to be neutral. They were the steam-engine, on or off the track—if on, carrying the blessings of a Christian civilization with marvelous rapidity into the hitherto unbroken forests; if off, precipitating a terrific destruction, the dismal sound of which is heard through the world, and will go down through succeeding ages. As they did, in one case at least, run off the track, we shall now pursue the immediate history of the melancholy affair, and shall try to show the true character of the victims who have at length been dragged from beneath the rubbish.

In the winter of 1691–92 a circle was formed in Salem Village for entertainment, and for practice in the black-arts. It consisted mostly of young girls, but had, as we shall see, some adult persons connected with it. It met in different private houses, and, among others, at the house of Mr. Parris, the Pastor.

The members of this circle, or "the afflicted persons," as they were called, are to appear so prominently in our story that the reader will be interested in an introduction to each one of them.

Mr. Parris had in his family two slaves, man and wife, whom he had brought from one of the Spanish West India Islands. The man was known as John Indian, and his wife as Tituba. They were members of the circle, or, at least, prompted its formation, and seemed to have supplied it with material for excitement from their knowledge of the superstitious stories and practices of their ignorant race.

Elizabeth, daughter of Mr. Parris, was nine years of age. She met in the circle and graduated into a brief course of public acting, after which she was removed by her father from the Village.

Abigail Williams, a niece of Mr. Parris, a member of his family, was eleven years of age; she drank fully of the spirit of the circle in her attendance, and exercised her acquisitions to the end of the witchcraft proceedings.

Ann Putnam, daughter of Sergeant Thomas Putnam, whose mother was Ann (Carr) Putnam, was twelve years old, and will become painfully well known to the reader, as will her mother, who acted a conspicuous part with her daughter in the bloody tragedies.

Mary Walcot, seventeen years old, belonged also to a good family, her father, Captain Jonathan Walcot, having acted as deacon of the parish for several years, though not a Church member.

Mary Lewis, aged seventeen, a servant-girl in the family of Rev. George Burroughs, and afterward of Thomas Putnam, was an eminent graduate of the circle.

Elizabeth Hubbard, also seventeen years of age, niece of the wife of Dr. Griggs, physician of the village, and a member of his household, proved her training in the circle by her subsequent distinguished acting.

Mary Warren, twenty years old, servant in the family of John Proctor, and Sarah Churchhill, also twenty, servant of George Jacobs, Sen., were badly eminent.

Besides Mrs. Ann Putnam, these girls had the co-operation of a Mrs. Pope, a woman by the name of Bibber, and an "ancient" lady by the name of Goodell.

During the winter the circle developed a facility for strange acting. They crept under benches and chairs, into holes, uttered piercing cries, were thrown into painful positions, fell down in terrible fits, and suffered agonizing tortures. The families where they met were of course alarmed. The neighborhood became excited, Dr. Griggs was called in, and, their case being out of the beaten track of his practice, he pronounced it a genuine type of witchcraft.

The girls grew bold from the attention paid them, and extended their operations to the social and public meetings. On Sunday, March 2, 1692, as Mr. Lawson, who occupied the pulpit that day, was about to rise to preach, Abigail Williams cried out, "Now stand up and name your text!" and added, when he had read it, "It's a long text."

When the preacher was in the midst of his sermon Mrs. Pope exclaimed, "Now, there is enough of that." When, in the afternoon, the preacher referred to the doctrine of the morning sermon, Abigail Williams shouted, "I know no doctrine you had. If you did name one I have forgot it."

An aged member of the Church was present against whom a warrant was then held for her apprehension as a witch. Abigail Williams called out her name in the public congregation, saying, "Look where she sits upon the beam, sucking her yellow-bird betwixt her fingers." Ann Putnam chimed in, "There is a yellow-bird sitting on the minister's hat, as it hangs on the pin in the pulpit."

The preacher persevered in the service in spite of these interruptions, no one restraining the girls. It was generally referred to "an evil hand," and the girls only pitied as "afflicted children." Let it be remembered that among those who took an opposite view and absented themselves from meeting were several members of the family of Francis Nurse. John Proctor, at a later period in their actings, said he should take his wench home (referring to his servant-girl, Mary Warren) and whip her. One cannot help wishing that the experiment of a whipping all round had been tried upon the girls just at this point, followed by their separation from each other at a distance from the Village. Instead of which they were soothingly addressed as "poor girls," and praying circles formed in their behalf, which might wisely have been preceded and followed by a scriptural use of the rod. Their symptoms growing worse, the ministers of the neighborhood were called in, and a day was spent by them in prayer at the parsonage. The children performed before their eyes to their amazement. Their judgment was that "an evil hand" was upon them. This, of course, was soon known far and wide, and the excited people flocked to see the dreadful exhibitions. The ground of the farmer remained untilled, and the work of the mechanic remained unperformed. The torch was already set to the inflammable materials, and no man could subdue the fire that was kindled. Bentley says: "The torrent of opinion was irresistible. They who thought they saw the delusion did not oppose it. They who were deluded were terrified into distraction."

The fundamental error of the witchcraft theory —that there must be a voluntary human agent through whom the devil was afflicting the girls and beginning his destruction of the substance and the souls of the people—was applied here, and the inquiry was whispered "with white lips," and passed through every family, "Who are the witches?"

This brings us to the sad history of the first victims.

CHAPTER VIII.

The First Victims.

"THE afflicted persons" began cautiously to utter the names of "Good," "Osburn," "Tituba." On the 29th of February, 1692, warrants were issued against them on the complaint of three of the most prominent men in the village, two of whom, at least, at a later period of the delusion, were among those who distrusted the wisdom of the proceedings.

The accused were duly indicted and brought forward for examination. All of the indictments are in much the same form. They charge the prisoners with "certain detestable arts called witchcrafts and sorceries, wickedly and feloniously used, practiced and exercised," by which the persons named were "tortured, afflicted, pined, consumed, wasted, and tormented."

On the first of March the two most distinguished magistrates of the vicinity, Jonathan Corwin and John Hathorne, came in their official capacity to Salem Village. They were from eminent families, were men whom their fellow-citizens had delighted to honor for their abilities, learning, and integrity. Though we may find them evidently prejudiced against those whom they came to examine, they were no more so, probably, than the most of the judges as well as people about them.

It was a memorable day when they rode into the village and reined up at Deacon Nathaniel Ingersoll's door, attended by sheriffs, marshals, and all the solemn pomp and impressive ceremony which then more than now were thrown about the movements of high officials.

The crowd was great, and the court adjourned from "the ordinary" to the meeting-house, which was filled with excited spectators, whose feverish emotions may be partially understood by those who crowded the public assemblies during the critical periods of the late war. The judges took their seats before a raised platform in front of the pulpit. Beside them was seated Ezekiel Cheever as secretary. No counsel appeared for the accused, and, in this case, no friends. They were already tried and condemned in the public mind. The court was opened by prayer, and the prisoners were brought forward. The officers on delivering them to the authorities said that they "had made diligent search for images and such like, but could find none."

Sarah Good was the first examined. She was a homeless, friendless, and wretched person, whose ignorant and weak husband had forsaken her, and whose children wandered with her from door to door begging their daily bread. If the devil were craftily and cautiously educating the Court and people to judicial recklessness in taking life, Sarah Good was fittingly selected as the first victim.

The following is the record of her trial made by Cheever. That made by Judge Hathorne does not differ in any facts.

"'Sarah Good, what evil spirit have you familiarity with?'

"'None.'

"'Have you made no contracts with the devil?'

"'No.'

"'Why do you hurt these children?'

"'I do not hurt them. I scorn it.'

"'Who do you employ, then, to do it?'

"'I employ no one.'

"'What creature do you employ, then?'

"'No creature; but I am falsely accused.'

"'Why did you go away muttering from Mr. Parris' house?'

"'I did not mutter; but I thanked him for what he gave my child.'

"'Have you made no contract with the devil?'

"'No.'

"Hathorne desired the children, all of them, to look upon her, and see if this were the person that hurt them; and so they all did look upon her, and said this was one of the persons that did torment them. Presently they were all tormented.

"Hathorne. 'Sarah Good, do you not see now what you have done? Why do you not tell us the truth? Why do you thus torment these poor children?'

"'I do not torment them.'

"'Who do you employ, then?'

"'I employ nobody. I scorn it.'

"'How came they thus tormented?'

"'What do I know? You bring others here, and now you charge me with it.'

"'Why, who was it?'

"'I do not know; but it was some you brought into the meeting-house with you.'

"'We brought you into the meeting-house.'

"'But you brought in two more.'

"'Who was it, then, that tormented the children?'

"'It was Osburn.'

"'What is it you say when you go muttering away from persons' houses?'

"'If I must tell you I will tell.'

"'Do tell us, then.'

"'If I must tell I will tell; it is the commandments. I may say my commandments, I hope.'

"'What commandment is it?'

"'If I must tell you I will tell you; it is a psalm.'

"'What psalm?'

"After a long time she muttered over some part of a psalm.

"'Who do you serve?'

"'I serve God.'

"'What God do you serve?'

"'The God that made heaven and earth.' (Though she was not willing to mention the word 'God.')

"Her answers were in a wicked, spiteful manner, reflecting and retorting against the authority with base and abusive words; and many lies she was taken in. It was here said that her husband had said that he was afraid that she either was a witch or would be one very quickly. The worshipful Mr. Hathorne asked him his reason why he said so of her, whether he had ever seen any thing by her. He answered, 'No, not in this nature, but it was her bad carriage to him; and indeed,' said he, 'I may say with tears that she is an enemy to all good.'"

Sarah Good was now removed from the meeting-house, and Sarah Osburn brought in. Osburn had been left a widow with two children by the death of her first husband, Robert Prince. Prince was a man of good family and considerable property, and left his wife and their children a farm, on which they lived. The widow, after a while, married her Irish laborer, Alexander Osburn. They were both, soon after, received into the Church; but for some reason she became the subject of scandal, became depressed, and for a long time previous to her arrest had been confined to her bed. The following is from Cheever's records of the trial:

"'What evil spirit have you familiarity with?'

"'None.'

"'Have you made no contract with the devil?'

"'No; I never saw the devil in my life.'

"'Why do you hurt these children?'

"'I do not hurt them.'

"'Who do you employ, then, to hurt them?'

"'I employ nobody.'

"'What familiarity have you with Sarah Good?'

"'None; I have not seen her these two years.'

"'Where did you see her, then?'

"'One day agoing to town.'

"'What communications had you with her?'

"'I had none, only "How do you do," or so. I do not know her by name.'

"'What did you call her, then?'

"(Osburn made a stand at that; at last said she called her Sarah.)

"'Sarah Good saith that it was you that hurt the children.'

"'I do not know that the devil goes about in my likeness to do any hurt.'

"Mr. Hathorne desired the children to stand up, and look upon her and see if they did know her, which they all did; and every one of them said that this was one of the women that did afflict them, and that they had constantly seen her in the very habit she was now in. Three evidences declared that she said this morning that she was more like to be bewitched than that she was a witch. Mr. Hathorne asked her what made her say so. She answered that she was frighted one time in her sleep, and either saw or dreamed that she saw a thing like an Indian, all black, which did pinch her in the neck, and pulled her by the back part of her head to the door of the house.

"'Did you never see any thing else?'

"'No.'

"(It was said by some in the meeting-house that she had said that she would never believe that lying spirit any more.)

"'What lying spirit is this? Hath the devil ever deceived you and been false to you?'

"'I do not know the devil. I never did see him.'

"'What lying spirit was it, then?'

"'It was a voice that I thought I heard.'

"'What did it propound to you?'

"'That I should go no more to meeting; but I said I would, and did go the next Sabbath-day.'

"'Were you never tempted further?'

"'No.'

"'Why did you yield thus far to the devil as never to go to meeting since?'

"'Alas, I have been sick and not able to go.'

"Her husband and others said that she had not been at meeting three years and two months.

Sarah Osburn was removed from the meeting-house, and the Indian slave Tituba took the stand. We shall see that she proved more yielding to the management of the court.

"'Tituba, what evil spirit have you familiarity with?'

"'None.'

"'Why do you hurt these children?'

"'I do not hurt them.'

"'Who is it, then?'

"'The devil for aught I know.'

"'Did you never see the devil?'

"'The devil came to me and bid me serve him.'

"'Who have you seen?'

"'Four women sometimes hurt the children.'

"'Who were they?'

"'Goody Osburn and Sarah Good, and I don't know who the others were. Sarah Good and Osburn would have me hurt the children, but I would not.'

" (She further said there was a tall man of Boston that she did see.)

" 'When did you see them?'

" 'Last night, at Boston.'

" 'What did they say to you?'

" 'They said, "Hurt the children."'

" 'And did you hurt them?'

" 'No; there is four women and one man; they hurt the children, and then they lay all upon me; and they tell me if I will not hurt the children they will hurt me.'

" 'But did you hurt them?'

" 'Yes, but will hurt them no more.'

" 'Are you not sorry you hurt them?'

" 'Yes.'

" 'And why, then, do you hurt them?'

" 'They say, "Hurt children or we will do worse to you."'

" 'What have you seen?'

" 'A man come to me and say, "Serve me."'

" 'What service?'

" 'Hurt the children; and last night there was an appearance which said, "Kill the children," and if I would not go on hurting the children they would do worse to me.'

" 'What is the appearance you see?'

" 'Sometimes it is like a hog, and sometimes like a great dog.'

" (This appearance she saith she did see four times.)

"'What did it say to you?'

"'The black dog said, "Serve me." But I said, "I am afraid." He said if I did not he would do worse to me.'

"'What did you say to it?'

"'I will serve you no longer. Then he said he would hurt me, and he looks like a man and threatens to hurt me.' (She said that this man had a yellow-bird that kept with him.) 'And he told me he had more pretty things that he would give me if I would serve him.'

"'What were these pretty things?'

"'He did not show me them.'

"'What else have you seen?'

"'Two cats: a red cat and a black cat.'

"'What did they say to you?'

"'They said, "Serve me."'

"'What service?'

"'She said, "Hurt the children."'

"'Did you not pinch Elizabeth Hubbard this morning?'

"'The man brought her to me and made me pinch her.'

"'Why did you go to Thos. Putnam's last night and hurt his child?'

"'They pull and haul me and make me go.'

"'And what would they have you do?'

"'Kill her with a knife.'

"(Lieutenant Fuller and others said at this time, when the child saw these persons and was tormented by them, that she did complain that they would have her cut her head off with a knife.)

"'How did you go?'

"'We did ride upon sticks and are there presently.'

"'Do you go through the trees or over them?'

'"We see nothing, but are there presently.'

"'Why did you not tell your master?'

"'I was afraid; they said they would cut off my head if I told.'

"'What attendants hath Sarah Good?'

"'A yellow-bird; and she would have given me one.'

"'What did she give it?'

"'It did suck her between her fingers.'

"'Did you not hurt Mr. Curren's child?'

"'Goody Osburn and Goody Good told that they did hurt Mr. Curren's child, and would have had me hurt him too, but I did not.'

"'What hath Sarah Osburn?'

"'Yesterday she had a thing with a head like a woman, with two legs and wings.'

"(Abigail Williams, that lives with her uncle, Mr. Parris, said that she did see the same creature, and it turned into the shape of Goody Osburn.)

"'What else have you seen with Osburn?'

"'Another thing, hairy; it goes upright like a man, it hath only two legs.'

"'Did you not see Sarah Good upon Elizabeth Hubbard last Saturday?'

"'I did see her set a wolf upon her to afflict her.'

"(The persons with this maid did say that she did complain of a wolf. She further said that she saw a cat with Good at another time.)

"'What clothes does the man go in?'

"'He goes in black clothes; a tall man with white hair, I think.'

"'How doth the woman go?'

"'In a white hood, and a black hood with a top-knot.'

"'Do you see who it is that torments these children now?'

"'Yes; it is Goody Good. She hurts them in her own shape.'

"'Who is it that hurts them now?'

"'I am blind now; I cannot see.'"

These examinations were repeated for several days, Good and Osburn steadily denying, and the Indian slave confessing what the judges term "the matter-of-fact." Each night the prisoners were sent to Ipswich jail, a distance of ten miles, and brought back in the morning. Osburn, in feeble health, well-nigh sunk under it; but Good retained her nimbleness of foot and tongue, leaping occasionally from her horse, and railing on the magistrates in good set terms. A more pious person might have been tempted to do so. On the seventh day the trial closed, and the three accused were sent to the Boston jail, and secured by special bars and fetters, as was deemed necessary, with a witch, in order to make confinement sure.

Tituba deserved some consideration at the hands of the judges, if the depositions of Samuel Parris, Thomas Putnam, and E. Cheever were true. They deposed that the poor girls were all set upon by the three accused during their examination. But when Tituba began to confess her shape ceased to torment, and she was herself tortured "before authority," in the very presence of the Judge, by some unseen agent of the cheated adversary.

Tituba lay in jail a year and a month, and was sold to pay the jail fees. Sarah Osburn remained in confinement nine weeks and two days, when death kindly released her.

We shall meet Sarah Good again.

CHAPTER IX.

The Accusers Strike Higher.

IT is plain, from the records presented in the previous chapter, that the Court and the mass of the people were in sympathy with the accusers. The Court showed this by the importance it attached to their testimony; the people, by their wondering attention in the crowded church, and the occasional volunteering of a testimony from their midst against the prisoners. Popular feeling, that august personage who is supposed to judge righteously, but is often sadly at fault, joined with the accusers. It was evident then, that if the Great Accuser was chief manager of this whole affair, he would deem it quite a safe stroke of policy to strike at higher game. A bed-ridden woman who could endure only nine weeks of imprisonment, and who could not wait to be hanged, but then died, a wretched beggar, and an ignorant slave, would answer as the first victims, but would not be worthy of the further progress of the grand tragedy.

Martha Corey next appears on the stage. We have introduced to the reader both Martha and her more distinguished husband in our chapter of "Portraits." Mrs. Corey seems to have been a woman of strong sense, a fair measure of intelligence, and genuine Christian experience. She turned away from the witchcraft proceedings from the beginning, doubting, at least, its claims to belief, and disapproving the trials. Her husband, on the other hand, was carried away with the current delusion. She is said to have hid his saddle, to prevent his attendance with the amazed crowd at the meeting-house. Longfellow beautifully pictures this incident:

COREY. Ho! Martha! Martha!
Have you seen my saddle?
MARTHA. I saw it yesterday.
COREY. Where did you see it?
MARTHA. On a gray mare that somebody was riding
Along the village road.
COREY. Who was it? Tell me.
MARTHA. Some one who should have stayed at home.
COREY, (*restraining himself,*) I see!
Don't vex me, Martha. Tell me where it is.
MARTHA. I've hidden it away.
COREY. Go fetch it me.
MARTHA. Go find it.
COREY. No. I'll ride down to the village
Bareback; and when the people stare and say,
"Giles Corey, where's your saddle?" I will answer,
"A witch has stolen it." How shall you like that?
MARTHA. I shall not like it.
COREY. Then go fetch the saddle. (*Exit* Martha)
MARTHA. (*Returning.*) There! There's the saddle.
COREY. Take it up.
MARTHA. I wont.
COREY. Then let it lie there. I'll ride to the village
And say you are a witch.
MARTHA. No, not that, Giles. (*She takes up the saddle.*)

COREY. Now come with me and saddle the gray mare
With your own hands, and you shall see me ride
Along the village road as is becoming
Giles Corey of the Salem Farms, your husband.

Giles Corey and wife had other small jars, which, not being strange nor important, would not have crept into history if they had not been dragged into Court. Somehow the old man's deposition was obtained concerning some matters which were supposed to bear against his wife, implying some witchcraft on her part. How "far-fetched" they were the reader will see. It is to this effect: One Saturday night, in attempting "duty"—a term by which family prayer was expressed—he had no liberty—could not utter his desires with any sense. His wife perceiving this drew near to him, after which, "in a little space," he did "according to his measure attend the duty." Giles also deposed that at one time one of his oxen lay down, and when he attempted to rise was as if "hip shot," but was soon all right. At another time his cat was taken suddenly and seriously ill, and his wife advised him to knock her in the head; but the cat recovered without the application of that remedy. The deposition closes with this serious allegation:

"My wife hath been wont to sit up after I went to bed, and I have perceived her to kneel down on the hearth, as if she were at prayer, but I heard nothing."

It will be remembered that Giles was an old man when he professed to be changed by grace and joined the Church. Before this he was a man of the world. This suggests the difficulty he had in praying, and is truthfully rendered by Longfellow:

COREY. I will not make believe! I say to-night
There's something thwarts me when I wish to pray,
And thrusts into my mind, instead of prayers,
Hate and revenge, and things that are not prayers;
Something of my old self—my old, bad life—
And the old Adam in me rises up
And will not let me pray. I am afraid
The devil hinders me. You know I say
Just what I think, and nothing more nor less,
And when I pray my heart is in my prayer;
I cannot say one thing and mean another.
If I can't pray I will not make believe.

Whisperings against Mrs. Corey as a witch being current, two prominent members of the Church, Edward Putnam and Ezekiel Cheever, proposed to visit her regarding the matter, which certainly was a becoming and Christian course; but they first visited Thomas Putnam's to consult his accusing, specter-seeing daughter, Ann, which did not appear so proper or Christian. Ann, as she affirmed, and as the committee were evidently inclined to believe, had been awfully tortured by Martha Corey, though her bodily presence was known not to have been near her. The committee inquired of Ann a description of the dress in which Mrs. Corey came to her. Ann replied that Goody Corey knew that they were about to make this visit, and had just appeared to her and blinded her, so that she could not see what clothes she wore.

The brethren visited Sister Corey and found her alone. She told them that she knew the occasion of their call, but said she was not a witch, and could not help people's talk. They told her that "the afflicted person" accused her. "Does she tell what clothes I have on?" inquired Mrs. Corey eagerly. When the visitors gave Ann's reasons for not knowing in what dress she came she smiled, and intimated that Ann had "showed them a pretty trick." They discoursed solemnly about the great wickedness of witchcraft, and were shocked at her indifference. She even intimated that she did not believe there were any witches.

Upon the whole the brethren were not favorably impressed with the evidence of the sister's innocence. Two days after this interview Martha Corey was brought to the house of Thomas Putnam, and at the sight of her Ann was shockingly handled. This was decisive, and the accused was arrested and brought before "authority." Her examination took place in the village meeting-house, March 21. Rev. Nicholas Noyes from the town opened the session with prayer, and Mr. Parris acted as scribe. The records exhibit the same method of examination as before on the part of the Court, but a harder subject to deal with, because more capable of answering for herself. The accused had, as did the others, many to cross-examine her, but none to cross question her accusers.

Mr. Hathorne. "You are now in the hands of

authority. Tell me, now, why you hurt these persons."

"I do not."

"Who doth?"

"Pray give me leave to go to prayer."

This request was made sundry times.

"We do not send for you to prayer; but tell me why you hurt these?"

"I am an innocent person; I never had to do with witchcraft since I was born. I am a gospel woman."

"Do not you see these complain of you?"

"The Lord open the eyes of the magistrates and ministers; the Lord show his power to discover the guilty!"

"Tell us who hurts these children?"

"I do not know."

"If you be guilty of this fact do you think you can hide it?"

"The Lord knows."

"Well, tell us what you know of this matter."

"Why, I am a gospel woman, and do you think I can have to do with witchcraft too?"

"How could you tell, then, that the child was bid to observe what clothes you wore when some came to speak with you?"

Cheever interrupted her and bid her not begin with a lie; and so Edward Putnam declared the matter.

Mr. Hathorne. "Who told you that?"

"He said the child said—"

CHEEVER. "You speak falsely."

Then Edward Putnam read again.

It will be remembered that Cheever and Putnam, who thus interrupt Corey and give her the lie, were the committee who visited her.

Mr. HATHORNE. "Why did you ask if the child told what clothes you wore?"

"My husband told me the others told."

"Who told you about the clothes? Why did you ask that question?"

"Because I heard the children told what clothes the others wore."

"Goodman Corey, did you tell her?"

The old man denied that he told her so.

"Did you not say your husband told you so?"

No answer.

"Who hurts these children? Now look upon them?"

"I cannot help it."

"Did you not say you would tell the truth why you asked that question? how came you to the knowledge?"

"I did but ask."

"You dare thus to lie in all this assembly. You are now before authority. I expect the truth; you promised it. Speak, now, and tell who told you what clothes?"

"Nobody."

"How came you to know that the children would be examined what clothes you wore?"

"Because I thought the child was wiser than any body if she knew."

"Give me an answer; you said your husband told you."

"He told me the children said I afflicted them."

"How do you know what they came for? answer me this truly; will you say how you came to know what they came for?"

"I had heard speech that the children said I troubled them, and I thought they might come to examine."

"But how did you know it?"

"I thought they did."

"Did not you say you would tell the truth? who told you what they came for?"

"Nobody."

"How did you know?"

"I did think so."

"But you said you knew so."

CHILDREN. "There is a man whispering in her ear."

Hathorne continued: "What did he say to you?"

"We must not believe all that these distracted children say."

"Cannot you tell what that man whispered?"

"I saw nobody."

"But did not you hear?"

"No."

Here was extreme agony of all the afflicted.

"If you expect mercy from God you must look for it in God's way, by confession. Do you think to find mercy by aggravating your sins?"

"A true thing."

"Look for it, then, in God's way."

"So I do."

"Give glory to God and confess, then?"

"But I cannot confess."

"Do not you see how these afflicted do charge you?"

"We must not believe distracted persons."

"Did not you say our eyes were blinded; you would open them?"

"Yes, to accuse the innocent."

"Why cannot the girl stand before you?"

"I do not know."

"What do you mean by that?"

"I saw them fall down."

"It seems to be an insulting speech, as if they could not stand before you?"

"They cannot stand before others."

"But you said they cannot stand before you. Tell me what was that turning upon the spit by you?"

"You believe the children that are distracted. I saw no spit. . . . What can I do? Many rise up against me."

"Why, confess."

"So I would if I were guilty."

There was much more of this kind of examination, if such it could be called, when the prisoner's guilt was assumed and her words perverted into evidence against her. The Judge returned with warmth again and again to the tender point where she said she would open the magistrates and ministers' eyes. The children occasionally interposed by declaring they saw "the yellow-bird," and then the "man whispering in her ear," varied by shrieks, from the suffering Corey inflicted. Rev. Mr. Noyes put in his word, saying, "I believe it is apparent she practices witchcraft in the congregation. There is no need of images."

While the Judge, "the afflicted girls," and the volunteers from the audience, were doing their part to prove to Martha Corey her witchcraft, (it was from the first plain to them,) the committee by whom she had been visited, Edward Putnam and Ezekiel Cheever, with the aid of the Secretary, Rev. Samuel Parris, were doing service in the same direction by obtaining evidence of her guilt from her lips, fingers, hands, feet, and breast. The criminality of her eyes in knocking down the children had been seen, as it was believed, by all. These men solemnly deposed that while upon her examination they "did see" her bite the children by biting her own lips; that wicked trick being discovered and stopped, they saw her pinch them by nipping her own fingers; that mischief prevented by confining her hands, she afflicted them by working her foot; this restrained, she pressed upon the seat with her breast, "and Mistress Pope was greatly afflicted by great pressure upon her stomach."

Such persistency in witchcraft in the presence "of authority," and the careful observers who testified, showed little sagacity on Martha Corey's part in self-preservation.

While thus beset on every hand, there is something quite moving in the exclamations forced from the oppressed prisoner—"You are all against me and I cannot help it!" "If you will all go hang me, how can I help it!" "What can I do when many rise up against me!" But the bitterest ingredient in her cup seems to have been the apparent sympathy of her husband with her accusers. One of his sons-in-law, too, joined in the clamor against her. But it will appear in the end that Giles Corey was entrapped into this opposition to his wife. He redeemed himself subsequently.

The judges, of course, sent Martha Corey to jail. They could not make her see her guilt as they saw it. But enough had been done to give fresh courage to the accusers. The most sacred ties were loosening in the society about Salem Village, and the Destroyer might strike at still more eminent victims.

CHAPTER X.

An Excellent Matron.

REBECCA NURSE was the wife of Francis Nurse. Her husband will be remembered as the owner of the Townsend Bishop Farm, and as the occupant of its fine mansion. The aged couple had secured their homestead by hard work and sterling integrity. Their sons and sons-in-law, with their wives and children, were settled about them —a thrifty, enterprising family, the members of which had, by the blessing of God, been the builders of their own fortunes. The parental home had been one of prayer, and the blessing of God lingered about it, while its influence extended in blessings to its children and children's children. Mrs. Nurse was of an excellent family, the Towns, and her brothers and other relatives had settled in and about Topsfield. Her sisters, Mary Easty and Sarah Cloyse, will be brought to our notice.

Francis Nurse and wife had, then, worldly substance, a wide circle of respected family connections and friends; and they possessed, what was better than these, a religious character. They could look back upon the past with satisfaction, and forward to the future with a hope that their declining sun would set without a cloud:

> "How vain are all things here below;
> How false, and yet how fair!"

Rebecca Nurse was now seventy-one years of age, and her husband probably older. The cloud, black and driven by a furious tempest, which was desolating Salem Village, came rushing down upon their quiet mansion. Some faithful friends, perceiving that it would take that direction, endeavored to turn it aside.

The graduates of the circle had muttered, with other names, Rebecca Nurse. Why they should have turned to so excellent a family, and a woman of such eminent repute for piety, can only be surmised. It was a common notion that the devil sought the confederacy of the wisest and best in the Church in order thus to do it the more injury, and that he bid high for such allies. Some suggest that a grudge was felt against them on account of their expressed disapproval of the conduct, in the church, of the afflicted girls, and that the relations of Mrs. Nurse to the "Topsfield men," and the complication of her family with the bitter border war with that town, afforded the occasion for attack. It is not easy to follow the evolutions of the witchcraft tempest.

One of the four friends who attempted to turn the storm from Rebecca Nurse was Elizabeth Porter, sister to John Hathorne, the presiding Judge. She with her husband and Peter Cloyse, Mrs.

Nurse's brother-in-law, and a well-to-do farmer of prominence by the name of Anderson, on hearing of the girls' whispers against her went to the house of Mrs. Nurse. They found her very feeble in body, having been sick a week. They inquired after her spiritual welfare, and were assured, with an exclamation of thanksgiving, that God had granted her an unusual measure of his presence during her sickness, and that she was "pressing toward the mark." She spoke with tenderness of the afflicted girls, especially those of Mr. Parris' family, said she was grieved for them, and would have called to express her sympathy but for ill health, and for fear of fits to which she had been subject; yet "her heart went to God for them." At this point the visitors delivered their unpleasant message: "We hear that you are named by them as a witch." The amazed matron remained for some moments silent, confounded, we may well suppose, by the announcement. She then meekly replied, "Well, if it be so, the will of the Lord be done." After another pause she added: "Well, as to this thing, I am as innocent as the child unborn; but surely, what sin hath God found out in me unrepented of, that he should lay such an affliction upon me in my old age."

The incidents of this interview were drawn out into a deposition, signed by the visitors, and presented, we suppose, for the consideration of the Court.

But Rebecca Nurse was arrested and brought to trial at the meeting-house. The crowd was greater and, if possible, more excited than ever. Mr. Hale of Beverly opened the Court with prayer. At the opening, some of the girls declared that the prisoner had never hurt them; among these was Mary Walcot. But soon Mary shouted out that Rebecca Nurse was biting her, and the marks of her teeth were shown on her wrist. Immediately the screeching and noise of the afflicted became terrific, so that it was heard by one who "walked a little distance from the meeting-house in the neighboring field," "so that the whole assembly was struck with consternation," "and were afraid that those who sat next to them were under the influence of witchcraft." It was under such circumstances that the trial of the aged invalid proceeded.

Mr. Hathorne. "What do you say," speaking to one afflicted, "that this woman has hurt you?"

"Yes, she hurt me this morning."

"Abigail, have you been hurt by this woman?"

"Yes."

Ann Putnam at this point cried out that she hurt her, and the Judge turned to the prisoner and said, "Goody Nurse, here are two, Ann Putnam, the child, and Abigail Williams, complain of your hurting them, what do you say to it?"

"I can say before my Eternal Father I am innocent, and God will clear my innocency."

Hathorne was more tender than on the former trial, and replied, "Here is never one in the assembly but desires it; but if you be guilty, pray God to discover you."

Just then Henry Kenney sprung to his feet in the congregation. The magistrate, always ready to permit such disorderly testifying, inquired what he had to say. He had a complaint against the prisoner, for he declared, "since this Nurse entered the house I have been seized twice with an amazed condition." It is to be hoped that Kenney felt better after delivering himself of such a complaint.

The Judge turned from this volunteer witness to the prisoner and declared that, in addition to what she had heard, Thomas Putnam's wife accused her of cruel treatment, to which Mrs. Nurse replied, "I am innocent and clear, and have not been able to get out of doors these eight or nine days."

Hathorne then called upon Edward Putnam, who seems to have testified to the sufferings of one of the afflicted by the prisoner.

When he had given "his relate," as the record says, the magistrate inquired, "Is this true, Goody Nurse?" The answer was prompt, the double negative being used for emphasis.

"I never afflicted no child, no, never in my life."

"You see these accuse you; is it true?"

"No."

"Are you an innocent person relating to this witchcraft?"

At this point Ann Putnam, the mother, put in one of her wild exclamations, "Did you not bring the Black Man with you? did you not bid me tempt God and die? How oft have you ate and drunk your own damnation?"

The suddenness of this appeal not only appalled

the congregation, but startled, by its terrific force and the solemn nature of its charges, the trembling prisoner. She threw up her hands and exclaimed, "God help me!"

Immediately, as persons are simultaneously struck by an electric shock, the afflicted were smitten with agonizing pains. "Do you see," said Hathorne, "what a solemn condition these are in? When your hands are loose these persons are afflicted."

Now two more of the circle troop come forward with their accusations, and Hathorne demands of Nurse what answer she has: "The Lord knows; I have not hurt them; I am an innocent person," she steadily replies.

Hathorne now puts in a solemn appeal:

"It is very awful for all to see these agonies, and you, an old professor, thus charged with contracting with the devil by the effects of it, and yet to see you stand with dry eyes when there are so many wet."

This sounds mean and insulting, to imply her indifference because an aged person like her, and under such agitation, could not weep. But it must be remembered that it was one item of the witchcraft theory that a witch could not weep. So the Judge was but insinuating her guilt before the assembly because of her dry eyes. Her answer was to the point, "You do not know my heart." And surely he as little knew the heart of her accusers.

The Judge persists, and says, "You would do

well, if you are guilty, to confess and give glory to God."

"I am as clear as the child unborn," is the reply.

The Judge continues, "Whatever certainty there may be in apparitions I know not, yet this with me strikes hard upon you, that you are at this very present charged with familiar spirits; this is your bodily person they speak to; they say now they see these familiar spirits come to your bodily person; now what do you say to that?"

"I have none."

After some more questioning of this kind, the Judge accuser changes his ground. He bethinks him of gossip about her sickness, and inquires, "How came you sick, for there is an odd discourse of that in the mouths of many?"

"I am sick at my stomach."

"Have you no wounds?"

"I have none but old age."

The magistrate, in the last question, refers to common talk about "witch marks" upon her person.

The girls at this point raise the cry of yellow-birds about her head and the black man whispering in her ear, and the Judge asks, "What do you say to it?"

"It is false; I am clear," is the emphatic reply.

"Possibly," suggests Hathorne, "you may apprehend you are no witch, but have you not been led aside by temptation that way?"

"I have not."

The Judge, apparently aside, says, "What a sad thing it is that a Church member here, and now another of Salem, should be thus accused and charged."

The Judge was startled from this soliloquy by Mrs. Pope, who went into a fit and shouted grievous accusations, followed by a general shriek from the circle, and fit prostrations.

The Judge returns to his insinuations about witch marks, and then changes base by asking, "Do you think these suffer voluntary or involuntary?"

"I cannot tell," is the cautious and charitable reply.

"That is strange; every one can judge."

"I must be silent," was the reply, which the magistrate takes up by remarking: "They accuse you of hurting them, and if you think it is not unwillingly, but by design, you must look upon them as murderers!"

"I cannot tell what to think of it," was the answer, which does not satisfy Hathorne, and he follows it up and finally puts it curtly: "Give an answer, now, do you think these suffer against their will or not?"

The answer was doubtless honest, but not pleasing: "I do not think these suffer against their wills."

Having received enough on that point, the Judge inquires: "Why did you never visit these afflicted persons?" Answer—"Because I was afraid I should have fits too."

Just here the accusers, on the motion of the body of the accused, put in evidence many and sore fits, and Hathorne exclaims: "Is it not an unaccountable case that when you are examined these persons are afflicted?" The answer is touchingly sad: "I have got nobody to look to but God."

When she moved her hands the girls were tortured, and Hathorne again demands: "Do you believe these afflicted persons are bewitched?"

"I do think they are."

Having received this emphatic answer, the Judge begins to expostulate:

"When this witchcraft came upon the stage there was no suspicion of Tituba, (Mr. Parris' Indian woman;) she professed much love for that child, Betty Parris; but it was her apparition did the mischief, and why should not you also be guilty, for your apparition doth hurt also." To which Nurse answered:

"Would you have me belie myself?"

Mrs. Nurse's head now drooped upon her shoulder, weary and faint no doubt, and immediately the afflicted felt their heads cruelly pressed to one side.

"Authority" now called upon Mr. Parris to read notes of what he had seen and heard of Thomas Putnam's wife while in her convulsive agonies. It was the old story of a terrific conflict with Rebecca Nurse's specter, in which Mrs. Putnam had received the most horrible torturing.

At the close of the solemn narration the magistrate turns to the prisoner and says, "What do you think of this?"

"I cannot help it; the devil may appear in my shape," was the reply.

A general confusion followed. Nurse held her head on one side, and one of the girls, Elizabeth Hubbard, "had her neck set in that posture." Whereupon Abigail Williams shouted, "Set up Goody Nurse's head! the maid's neck will be broke!" Mrs. Nurse's head was righted, and "Aaron Wey said that Betty Hubbard's was immediately righted."

The violent shrieks and shouts of the circle company, and the talking of many others, all doubtless testifying against the aged matron, made it impossible for the scribe to make a full record of the proceedings, and he says that, on this account, many things were omitted—such omissions being quite as well, no doubt, for the credit of the Court.

Though the prisoner was thus surrounded by those who assumed her guilt, there was one ingredient of bitterness, in the cup of sorrow put to Martha Corey's lips, which Rebecca Nurse did not taste—her family were not against her. They were true to her, and to their convictions of her innocence.

The commitment of this excellent person to prison after such evidence that she was in confederacy with the world's great enemy was a matter of course. Her limbs were loaded with chains, and her person put into the custody of the jailer.

Rebecca Nurse's trial was followed by that of Dorcas Good, a child not five years old. Marshal Herrick, a man of commanding presence, seemed to think such an arrest beneath his dignity, for she was brought in by a deputy. But the marshal, who had brought to Court an invalid old lady, a half-demented beggar, and an ignorant Indian slave-woman, could well have afforded to arrest a little girl.

Dorcas' conduct was certainly very wrong if the circle were to be credited; for they charged her with biting, pinching, pricking, and choking them, both before and at the trial, they showing the pins with which she pricked, and the prints of her teeth on their arms. She was sent to prison.

In the Boston jailer's bill against the Commonwealth, left on record, there is a charge of ten shillings for "two blankets for Sarah Good's child." We are glad to add that little Dorcas was not hanged.

CHAPTER XI.

The Voice of the Watchmen.

THERE was a significant evolution of the witchcraft tempest, beginning about the time of the trials of which we have thus spoken. Deodat Lawson will be remembered as one of the Pastors of the Village Church, who had left on the account of the parish contentions, and who while with them had buried a wife and daughter. He had married again and settled in Scituate. He returned to the Village on the 19th of March, the day on which Martha Corey was arrested. His coming seems to have been in accordance with a prearrangement, and he became the guest of Deacon Ingersoll. On the very day of his arrival he received a call from Mary Walcot, who astonished him by being seized and tortured on the spot by the witches. But the revelation, that most filled him with horror, was her declaration that his wife and daughter had been murdered by the wretches who were now being brought to justice. He probably refers to this testimony, as given afterward in Court, in his statement published at a later date, in which he says, speaking of the girls: "They did affirm at the examination, and again at the trial of an accused person . . . that they saw the ghosts of my wife and daughter, (who died above three years before,) and they did affirm that when the very ghosts looked on the prisoner at the bar they looked red, as if the blood would fly out of their faces with indignation."

With such information weighing upon his mind (for he seems to have received it as truth not to be called in question) he visits Mr. Parris, whose niece is tortured in his presence. The following Sunday he preaches with various interruptions from the circle. Monday Mrs. Corey is on trial in the meeting-house, and he hears the ghostly evidence of her guilt. He also sees her smite down her accusers with a look, deliver them from their fits by a touch, torture them in a variety of ways, though not near them, by simply reclining her head upon her shoulder, pressing her foot upon the floor, squeezing her fingers together, and, when these were prevented, pressing her breast against a seat. On Wednesday, the day of Rebecca Nurse's arrest, his mind is renewedly stimulated by a visit to Mrs. Ann Putnam. He found her bodily condition truly pitiable. At times her mouth was drawn up on one side, and her body strained, her convulsions lasting half an hour. But her mental condition was even worse, from violent conflicts with the great Enemy in the specter form of a witch. With much effort, and after many convulsions, she designated the third chapter of Revelation as that which Mr. Lawson should read. No sooner was the reading commenced than she was well, listening quietly to the Word, resting in her husband's arms.

Thursday morning Mr. Lawson witnessed the witchcraft exhibitions at the trial of Rebecca Nurse, and then walked the adjacent field in solemn meditation, but within the sound of the battle that was raging in the meeting-house. It was lecture day and he was to preach. The events that were transpiring had put the whole country astir, and excitement was at fever heat. It was a great occasion, requiring great fitness of heart and mind, but Mr. Lawson was master of the situation. He chose his text from Zechariah iii, 2: "The Lord rebuke thee, O Satan! even the Lord that hath chosen Jerusalem, rebuke thee; is not this a brand plucked out of the fire?"

He speaks of the great power of Satan over the bodies and souls of men, quoting many passages of Scripture. He illustrates his position by a reference to the afflicted. He says: "And whosoever hath observed these things must needs be convinced that the motions of the persons afflicted, both as to the manner and as to the violence of them, are the mere effects of diabolical malice and operations, and that it cannot rationally be imagined to proceed from any other source."

He fully indorses the claim which lay at the foundation of the witchcraft theory; he says: "He (Satan) contracts and indents with witches and wizards, that they shall be the instruments by whom he may more affect and afflict the bodies and minds of others; and if he can prevail upon those who make a visible profession, it may be a better covert unto his diabolical enterprise, and may the more readily pervert others to consenting unto his subjection."

He modestly puts forth the popular belief that witches make witches by inducing their victims to sign a book. He says, "So far as we can look into those hellish mysteries, and guess at the administration of the kingdom of darkness, we may learn that witches make witches by persuading one the other to subscribe to a book, or articles," etc.

In his application he exhorts his hearers to have sympathy with the afflicted, "those poor afflicted persons that are, by divine permission, under the direful influence of Satan's malice." He exclaims, "O pity, pity them!"

He makes a solemn and truly eloquent appeal to those in the congregation who may have entered into the diabolical covenant. At the naming of this he exclaims in the language of the prophet, "Be astonished, O ye heavens, at this, and be horribly afraid; be ye very desolate, saith the Lord!" He exhorts them to repentance, and warns them of the certain and fearful retributions of the judgment day if they do not. His appeals to Christians as to the manner and spirit of their resistance to the satanic assaults are truly scriptural, and fervently put: "I am this day commanded to call and cry an alarm unto you: ARM, ARM, ARM! . . . let us admit no parley, give no quarter; let none of Satan's forces or furies be more vigilant to hurt us, than we are to resist and oppress them, in the name and by the spirit, grace, and strength of our Lord Jesus Christ." He affirms that prayer is the great, all-efficient weapon for the emergency, and closes an exhortation to this duty thus: "What, therefore, I say unto one I say unto all, PRAY, PRAY, PRAY!"

His address to the magistrates who sat before him was modest and Christian. He exhorts them to "check and rebuke Satan," "by all ways and means that are according to the rule of God," reminding them that they "judge not for men but God." His deep sympathy in one direction would not allow him to close this word to the judges without saying, "Be a father to the poor; to these poor afflicted persons, in pitiful and painful endeavor to help them." It would have been well if he had added, "Be just to the poor, suffering, wronged, and outraged accused persons." But he did not see them in this light.

He appropriately closes the sermon by comforting believers with the truth "that the Lord Jesus, that captain of our salvation, hath already overcome the devil. . . . Hence, if we are by faith united to him, his victory is an earnest and prelibation of our conquest at last."

The sermon is considerably mixed. It indorses the whole witchcraft theory as it lay in the popular mind; it put forth extreme statements of his own theological faith on a much controverted doctrine of the Christian Church, in a connection which seemed to vindicate, as according to the will of

God, the worst things in this whole history; but it taught much wholesome Christian truth in a spirit truly that of a man who, though deluded in common with the masses about him, had the saving grace of God.

We have examined this sermon with deep interest, especially that part in which he addresses the judges, for some word on the character of these spectral testimonies. This was the vital point—the true topic of the occasion, in comparison with which all others were idle words. He commends the judges "to the rule of God" in judging. There were *a few* in the congregation who waited with breathless suspense for him to inquire, Is the declaration of a specter to be taken as teaching God's rules? If he had attacked specter evidence boldly, and with the ability and strength of conviction that pervades the sermon, our history might have ended here. But he would have encountered the raging storm, instead of being borne along and stimulated by it. What his belief was, on that point, we can only infer. The following extracts, from a preface to an edition of his sermon published by him in London years afterward, may enlighten us in this matter, and also show what the alleged preternatural facts were, which now bewildered and which continued for some months to bewilder the people:

"Some of the afflicted, as they were striving in their fits in open court, have (by invisible means) had their wrists bound together by a real cord, so as it could hardly be taken off without cutting.

Some afflicted have been found with their arms tied, and hanged upon a hook from whence others have been forced to take them down, that they might not expire in that posture.

"Some afflicted have been drawn under beds and tables by undiscerned force, so they could hardly be pulled out; and one was drawn half-way over the side of a well, and was, with much difficulty, recovered back again.

"Sometimes, in their fits, they have had their tongues drawn out of their mouths to a fearful length, their heads turned very much over their shoulders; and while they have been so strained in their fits, and had their arms, and legs, etc., wrested as if they were quite dislocated, the blood hath gushed plentifully out of their mouths for a considerable time together, which some, that they might be satisfied that it was real blood, took upon their finger and rubbed on their other hand. I saw several together thus violently strained and bleeding in their fits.

"A young woman that was afflicted at a fearful rate had a specter appear to her with a white sheet wrapped about it, not visible to the standers-by until the sufferer (violently striving in her fit) snatched at, took hold of, and tore off a corner of that sheet. Her father, being by, endeavored to lay hold of it with her, that she might retain what she had gotten; but, at the passing away of the specter, he had such a violent twitch of his hand as it would have been torn off; immediately thereupon appeared in the sufferer's hand the corner of a sheet—a real cloth visible to the spectators—which (as it is said) remains still to be seen."

Mr. Lawson's sermon was immediately printed, indorsed by the Boston ministers, and dedicated to the presiding magistrates, and the Pastors of the mother Church at Salem.

The Sabbath following the delivery of this rousing sermon was the regular communion Sabbath. Mr. Parris came on with a sermon, following up the vigorous blows of Mr. Lawson. Its drift and spirit may be judged by its text and title: "Christ knows how many devils there are in his Church, and who they are." John vi, 70, 71: "Jesus answered them, Have not I chosen you twelve, and one of you is a devil? He spake of Judas Iscariot the son of Simon: for he it was that should betray him, being one of the twelve."

Sarah Cloyse, a younger sister of Rebecca Nurse, was present with her husband. Her heart was, of course, almost crushed by the occurrences of the past week, but she had come under much constraint to commune with God's people at his Supper. The text, and the allusions to the recent events, were too much for her. She rose and left the meeting, the door slamming after her. It was said that a strong wind was blowing at the time, and that the slamming was purely accidental. It might have been considered diabolical, for it was a missile sent after the burdened woman which was barbed with death.

Such was the maddened state of public feeling

around Salem Village about the beginning of April, 1692, and such were some of the circumstances which stimulated it. It fully warranted the Arch-Manager, and those "possessed" persons through whom he wrought, in a change of base, which was skillfully effected, and the introduction soon after of a new tactic.

CHAPTER XII.

A Change of Base.

ON Monday, April 4, two of the chief men of the Village went to Salem and complained of Sarah Cloyse and Elizabeth Proctor to the magistrates, Hathorne and Corwin. The ground of complaint was, of course, "Sundry acts of witchcraft." On Monday, the eleventh, they were brought by the marshal, just before noon, to the meeting-house of Salem, which was larger than that at the Village, and was already crowded with a waiting, excited people. The Court was in waiting, not the court of two magistrates, as at the Village, but an imposing "Council" composed of the highest dignitaries of the colony. The record designates it as "a Council held at Salem," composed of "Thomas Danforth, Esq., Deputy Governor; James Russell, John Hathorne, Isaac Addington, Major Samuel Appleton, Captain Samuel Sewall, and Jonathan Corwin, Esquires."

Here were the Lieutenant Governor, Danforth, as Chief-justice, and six "assistants"—two from Boston, one from Charlestown, one from Ipswich, and two of Salem—representatives of the highest judiciary of the Commonwealth. From such a base the witchcraft operations took a wider range, and ceased to be a Salem Village affair. It was like Grant abandoning his intrenchments at Arlington Heights, and spreading his forces about Richmond. The heart of the colony was advantageously attacked. To assemble this Council for merely commitment trials was curious and significant. When the persons who were "committed" by this Court were tried for their lives it was before a subordinate one, reversing the order of usage and equity. But our whole history is curious and significant.

The Governor at this time was Simon Bradstreet, now eighty-seven years old, yet clear in intellect and sound at heart, a great and good man. On account of his great age, Danforth was acting Governor. This was unfortunate, for Danforth was an early and warm abettor of the delusion, (though he lived to see and confess his error,) while Bradstreet disapproved it throughout.

The Council being ready, in its impressive dignity, the audience on tip-toe of expectation, the amazed prisoners, Mrs. Cloyse and Mrs. Proctor, at the bar, the examination commenced. The first witness well became the character of the prosecution. John Indian, Mr. Parris' ignorant slave, husband of Tituba, one of the founders and instructors of the circle, steps forward. His master, who is scribe of the Council, puts the questions in the presence of "Authority."

"John, who hurt you?"

"Goody Proctor first, and then Goody Cloyse."

"What did she do to you?"

"She brought the book to me."

"John, tell the truth; who hurt you? Have you been hurt?"

"The first was a gentlewoman I saw."

"Who next?"

"Goody Cloyse."

"But who hurt you next?"

"Goody Proctor."

"What did she do to you?"

"She choked me and brought the book."

"How oft did she come to torment you?"

"A good many times; she and Goody Cloyse."

"Do they come to you in the night as well as in the day?"

"They come most in the day."

"Who?"

"Goody Cloyse and Goody Proctor."

"Where did she take hold of you?"

"Upon my throat to stop my breath."

"Do you know Goody Cloyse and Goody Proctor?"

"Yes, here is Goody Cloyse."

At this point Mrs. Cloyse demanded of her accuser—with indignation, we may well suppose—"When did I hurt thee?"

John answered, "A great many times."

"O, you are a grievous liar!" she replied, and the Council proceeded: "What did this Goody Cloyse do to you?"

"She pinched and bit me till the blood came."

"How long since this woman came and hurt you?"

"Yesterday, at meeting."

"At any time before?"

"Yes, a great many times."

When John Indian left the witness stand two of the girls were brought forward in turn. Mary Wolcot's testimony was of the customary material, alternated with bodily distortions with which she was tormented, and out of which she was brought by being brought in contact with one of the prisoners.

The questioner next demanded of Abigail Williams whether she had seen a company eat and drink at Mr. Parris' house?

"Yes, sir, that was in the sacrament."

"How many were they there?"

"About forty, and Goody Cloyse and Goody Good were their deacons."

"What was it?"

"They said it was our blood, and they had it twice that day."

Frequent allusions are made throughout the trials to these witch sacraments. Mr. Lawson's statement of what he heard in court concerning them will make their character plainer:

"Being brought to see the prisoners at the bar upon their trials, they did affirm in open court (I was then present) that they had oftentimes seen them at witch meetings, where was feasting, dancing, and jollity, as also at devil-sacraments; and particularly as they saw such a man —— amongst the rest of the cursed crew, and affirmed that he did administer the sacrament of Satan to them, encouraging them to go on in their way, and they should certainly prevail."

The witches had the sacrament of baptism also according to the testimony that Mr. Lawson had heard in court: "They affirmed that many of those wretched souls had been baptized at Newbury Falls, and at several other rivers and ponds; and, as to the manner of administration, the Great Officer of hell took them up by the body, and, putting their heads into the water, said over them, 'Thou art mine; I have full power over thee.'"

The Court having obtained Abigail's testimony concerning the diabolical sacrament, turned to Mary Walcot for a pleasanter kind; but what it had to do with the case in hand it is not easy to see, except, it may be, to relieve the general dismal story of the witness:

"Have you seen a white man?"

"Yes, sir, a great many times."

"What sort of a man was he?"

"A fine, grave man; and when he came, he made all the witches tremble."

Abigail Williams confirmed the fact concerning the white man, naming the place where they saw him—a very appropriate place—at Deacon Ingersoll's.

Mr. Lawson gives more details concerning what the witnesses said of the white man: "Some of them have at sundry times seen a *white man* appearing among the specters, and as soon as he appeared the *black witches* vanished. They said this white man had often foretold them what respite they should have from their fits, as sometimes a day or two or more, which fell out accordingly. One of the afflicted said she saw him, in her fit, and was with him in a glorious place which had no candle nor sun, yet was full of light and brightness, where there was a multitude in white, glittering robes, and they sang the song in Rev. v, 9; Psalm cx, cxlix. She was loath to leave that place, and said: '*How long shall I stay here? Let me be along with you.*' She was grieved she could stay no longer in that place and company."

At the close of the testimony concerning the white man seen at Deacon Ingersoll's, the Court asked, "Who was at Deacon Ingersoll's then?" meaning who of the witches whose presence the white man drove away. The answer was: "Goody Cloyse, Goody Nurse, Goody Corey, and Goody Good."

Mrs. Cloyse on hearing this asked for water, and sat down "as one seized with a dying, fainting fit." The girls immediately went into their agonies, some of them breaking in upon the tumult with the shout: "O, her spirit has gone to prison to her sister, Nurse," putting in, for variations, "There is the black man whispering in Cloyse's ear!" "There is a yellow bird flying round her head!" John Indian did the floor-tumbling and rolling about, at which he was expert by practice.

Order being restored, Mrs. Elizabeth Proctor was brought forward. Her husband, John Proctor, we have introduced to the reader as a straightforward, earnest, honest, plain-spoken man, of true courage. From the beginning to the end of his wife's wrongs, at the mouths of her accusers he was, as far as possible, at her side, to comfort and aid her, at the peril of his own life.

The first three of the circle who were addressed by the Court concerning the prisoner were dumb, one of them having her fist thrust into her mouth, where it would have been well for all of them to have kept their fists while in court. But John Indian was on his feet again with a loosened tongue. He declared Goody Proctor hurt him, to which she replied: "I take God in heaven to be my witness that I know nothing of it, no more than the child unborn." Then the girls' tongues were set at liberty and they cried against her, confirming their testimony with fits.

Abigail Williams, turning to Mrs. Proctor, said: 'Did you not tell me your maid had written?" to which Proctor mildly replied, "Dear child, it is not so. There is another judgment, dear child."

But kindness was lost upon the "dear child," for she went into a fit, and, coming out of it, joined with Ann Putnam in shouting, "Look you! there is Goody Proctor upon the beam." Whether the indignant husband, who was at his wife's side, gave the girls at this point "a piece of his mind," which was known to have a sharp edge and to cut deep, we do not know. It would have been like him. But the records say that they cried out against him, saying he was a wizard, which they proved by their fits, rendered on the spot. They shouted also, "There is Proctor going to take up Mrs. Pope's feet," and the record adds, "Her feet were immediately taken up," which proved, we suppose, the truth of the accusation. John Proctor when appealed to declared, of course, that he "knew nothing of it," that he was "innocent."

A circumstance of an original character occurred at Elizabeth Proctor's trial: "Abigail Williams and Ann Putnam both made offer to strike at said Proctor; but when Abigail's hand came near it opened, whereas it was made up into a fist before, and came down exceeding lightly as it drew near to said Proctor, and, at length, with open and extended fingers touched Proctor's hood very lightly. Immediately Abigail cried out, 'My fingers! my fingers! my fingers burn,' and Ann Putnam took on most grievously of her head and sunk down."

Judge Sewall wrote in his Journal, "It was awful to see how the afflicted girls were agitated," adding in the margin afterward, regretfully, "*Væ*," thrice repeated—"Alas, alas, alas!"

The tragic scene closed by the commitment of Sarah Cloyse and John Proctor and wife to Boston jail. The accused had gained nothing by the change of base, but, as was intended by the manager, "the possessed" stood on higher ground, where they could better survey the field of battle, and command its forces. This position secured and held, they fell back upon Salem Village to put into operation a new strategy.

On the 19th of April Giles Corey and Mary Warren of Salem Farms, Abigail Hobbs of Topsfield, and Bridget Bishop of Salem, were brought by the marshal to the house of Deacon Ingersoll under arrest "for high suspicion of witchcraft." The reader will recognize Corey and Mrs. Bishop as old acquaintances. Mary Warren, the servant girl of John Proctor, has thus far accompanied us as one of the "circle" experts, and a most relentless accuser. How came she under arrest, and what "is in the wind," when "the afflicted" are turning witches?

Mary had begun to see other visions than those in which specters flit; the sight of real girls—afflicted ones—dissembling, as she affirmed. She was reported as saying that, "The magistrates might as well examine Keyser's daughter, that has been distracted many years, and take notice of what she says, as well as any of the afflicted persons. For," she added, "when I was afflicted I thought I saw the apparitions of a hundred persons, for my head was turned and I could not tell what I said." And she further declared that since she had recovered she could not say that she saw any of the apparitions "at the time aforesaid."

No sooner had Mary begun to see this kind of vision, than her old circle companions began to see her in apparition afflicting them. She appeared in court as a prisoner, and it was rendered unto her as she had rendered unto others. Her guilt was demonstrated by ghostly sights and frightful convulsions on the part of the circle. This point reached, she returns into her old habit of falling into fits, and while she lay in one the circle cried out that she was going to confess. But forthwith they see Goody Corey, Proctor and wife, with spectral audacity, step in and strike her back to the floor as she attempts to rise and confess. Now comes Mary's heroic struggle, she rising up and exclaiming, "I will speak! O, I am sorry for it! I am sorry for it!" wringing her hands, moving to tears, no doubt, the amazed beholders, as they see her smitten to the floor again. On making another effort to speak, her teeth are set and she is convulsed. Presently she moans, "O Lord, help me! O good Lord, save me!"

She cries again, "I will tell, I will tell!" succeeded by fits; and then again, "I will tell, I will tell; they brought me to it." After this she is for some time overcome, and has to be carried out of court. When brought back and examined before the magistrates and ministers only, she was able to say, "She said, 'I shall not speak a word.' But I will, I will speak, Satan! She saith she will kill me. O, she saith she owes me a spite, and will claw me off. Avoid, Satan! for the name of God, avoid! Will ye? I will prevent ye in the name of God."

She was afterward several times examined in prison, the Enemy, as it was believed, interrupting her efforts to break her covenant with him, and thus the struggle went on until the middle of May, when Mary Warren succeeded in freeing her mind, making a full confession of all the particulars of her terrible fall, her dark conspiracy against Christ and his kingdom with the Prince of Darkness, and her hard-fought battles and her hair-breadth escape. She was soon set at liberty by authority, and henceforth Mary Warren is seven-fold more "possessed" and an accuser than before. The records will bring her forth as a principal witness against at least ten persons, all of whom were committed, and seven died by the hand of the executioner.

CHAPTER XIII.

Marked Cases.

THE arrest of Giles Corey might have been expected. He was made of such material, and had lived such a life, especially through his earlier years, as to afford occasion to the circle to accuse him of witchcraft. Besides, though at first giving testimony which was used against his wife, he had, on mature reflection, and on seeing her alarming situation, fallen back to her side. Now that he stands before authority in the meeting-house at Salem Village, the object of wonder, if not of indignation, from a gazing crowd; of bitter accusations which he knows to be false; and of assumed guilt on the part of an overbearing Court, he is self-possessed and deeply solemn. The current declaration of the accused came with emphasis from his lips: "I know nothing of it; I am innocent." The circle performed against him with unabated vigor, notwithstanding the defection of one of their number. They received the usual number of pinches, strangulations, threats, and seducements, from the accused. His feet, hands, eyes, head, and looks, inflicted the customary tortures upon the girls, in the very face of the people and their "worships," the magistrates. At one time his audacity in this direction was more than the meekness of the judge could endure, and he exclaimed,

"What! is it not enough to act witchcraft at other times, but must you do it now in the face of authority?"

Corey calmly replied, "I am a poor creature, and cannot help it."

But the motion of his head at the same instant tortured the heads and necks of the girls, and the magistrate broke forth in wrath again, "Why do you tell such lies against witnesses?"

The accusers tried to make a point of the disagreement of Corey and his wife. But he insisted that they had no contention except on a matter of opinion. He had in his family devotions used the phrase, "dying to sin and living to God." She thought it improper language; he contended that it was all right.

A less serious accusation urged against him was this: he said that he had seen the devil in the shape of a black hog, and was very much frightened.

"What did you see in the cow-house? Why do you deny it?" demands the judge.

"I saw nothing but my cattle," replies the prisoner.

The accusers urge the point renewedly, and the judge inquires, "What was it frightened you?"

The insinuation of cowardice stung the old man, and he replies, "I do not know that I ever spoke the word in my life."

Giles Corey being clearly entitled to commitment, in the opinion of the Court, another equally original character is brought forward—Bridget Bishop. The reader will recollect her in our "portraits of notable persons." Her "shovel-board," peculiar dress, unguarded speech, and resolute, if not at times severe temper, gave her a notoriety not altogether creditable. Yet no serious accusation had been proved against her. From the charge of witchcraft previously brought against her it will be recollected that she had been acquitted. But she is not likely to fare so well now. On her introduction to the Court she is met by the decisive testimony of the convulsions of the girls. Hathorne thus addresses her: "Bridget Bishop, you are now brought before authority to give account of what witchcraft you are conversant with?"

She turned away from the judge, and, looking upon the listening assembly, answered, "I take all this people to witness that I am clear."

Hathorne inquires of the accusing girls if she had hurt them. He then says to the prisoner, "You are here accused by four or five for hurting them. What do you say to it?"

"I never saw these persons before, nor I never was in this place before."

Mary Walcot steps forward with a special kind of proof of Bridget Bishop's guilt. She declares that her brother Jonathan had attacked Bridget's "appearance," and "tore her coat" in the conflict. Mary "heard it tear," so the point was clear to her mind. The prisoner, fortunately, had the identical coat on, and the Court, with gravity, no doubt, and becoming caution in reference to such evidence, ordered it to be examined on the spot, and, "upon some search a rent that seems to answer what was alleged was found."

The Court returns to the examination: "They say you bewitched your first husband to death."

"If it please your worship, I know nothing of it."

Mrs. Bishop shakes her head and the afflicted are shaken; again, she nods and they are tortured.

One testifies at this point that she said that she had been accounted a witch for ten years, but that she was no witch; and that the devil could not hurt her.

"I am no witch," interposes Bridget.

"Why, if you have not wrote in the book, tell me," says Hathorne, "how far you have gone."

"I have no familiarity with the devil."

"How is it then that your appearance doth hurt these?"

"I am innocent."

"Why, you seem to act witchcraft before us by the motion of your body, which seems to have influence upon the afflicted."

"I am innocent. I know not what a witch is."

This last expression the Judge seizes, and attempts to confound the prisoner with it: "How do you know then that you are not a witch?"

"I do not know what you say."

"How can you know you are not a witch, and yet not know what a witch is?"

"I am clear; if I were such a person you should know it."

The girls repeated the charge of murder against the prisoner, and Hathorne asks: "What do you say of those murders you are charged with?"

"I hope I am not guilty of murder."

Every one about Bridget seems to have interposed with confounding questions; Marshal Herrick put in his word, and the girls theirs, and Hathorne demanded if she could not find it in her heart to tell the truth. When he asked her if she had not heard that some had confessed, she answered, "No;" immediately two men stepped forward and declared they told her some had confessed. She simply answered, "I did not hear you." But the records say, "Here she is taken in a plain lie." Every thing is made to tell against the prisoner, and as the officers carry her away to prison the circle confirm the whole by great agonies.

It will be noticed that accusations of witchcraft were often fastened upon several members of the same family. Husbands and wives, parents and children, were overwhelmed together. This became especially painful when one member of a family turned accuser of other members.

William Hobbs, an early settler in the extreme northern portion of the Village territory, was a marked victim in this respect. He was now fifty years of age, having felled the forest, toiled on the recovered land, built him a home, and seen his children arrive at mature age. His life had been without reproach, so far as is known, and his sun, having passed its meridian, promised to set upon his well-earned forest home with golden rays. But clouds of inky blackness suddenly shut it from sight.

His daughter Abigail had for some time seemed deranged, wandering in the woods by night, and leading an aimless life. Persons testified that she had boasted that she was not afraid of any thing; that she had sold herself, soul and body, "to the Old Boy;" that she did not care what any body said to her, for she had seen the devil and made a covenant or bargain with him.

After Abigail's arrest, and she had been put face to face with "their worships," in Salem prison, April 20, she declared to them that an old acquaintance, named Judah White, had appeared to her in apparition, with Sarah Good, advising her to fly and not go to examination; that if she did go to examination not to confess. This Judah White was dressed "in fine clothes, in a sad-colored silk mantle, with a top-knot and hood;" that the devil, in the shape of a man, came to her, and would have her afflict the children; and brought their images in wood, and gave her thorns with which to prick these images, which, when she had done, Ann Putnam and her circle friends were pricked, and cried out for pain. She further enlightened the magistrates concerning a diabolical sacrament, attended by all the witches, in Mr. Parris' pasture, when she eat the "red bread and drank the red wine."

On the credit of this confession, Abigail became

a capital witness, and her perverse tongue was used against persons of unblemished character, among whom were her parents.

Mrs. Deliverance Hobbs, mother of Abigail, when placed before "authority," declared her innocence, deplored the sad condition of her daughter, and vainly hoped to be believed. But her daughter and the circle poured upon her defenceless head their unanswerable proof of guilt, supported by the sympathy of the Court and gaping crowd, the most of whom frowned upon the trembling prisoner. Abigail Williams and Mary Walcot declared that she "bit Mary's foot," and forthwith fell into a fit; John Indian said she had choked him. The magistrate assumes the truth of testimony from such high authority and demands, "Why do you hurt these persons?" "How come you to commit acts of witchcraft?" "Is it you or your appearance? how comes this about?" and the very pertinent question for a prisoner to answer: "Who hurts them if you do not?" To all Mrs. Hobbs answers steadily for awhile, "I know nothing of it;" "I have not consented to it that they should be hurt; no, in the sight of God and man, as I shall answer another day."

The witnesses persisted in their accusations, the Court in its assumptions, the crowd in its frowns; they all held out, but Mrs. Hobbs' strength of body and mind did not. She exclaimed, as Hathorne pressed his leading questions, "I am amazed." Henceforth she answered as her prosecutors—her persecutors—wished. She was a confessing witch, and another weapon had been wrenched from unwilling hands with which to smite down other victims.

Under such circumstances was William Hobbs, the husband and father, brought before the judges. The girls declared he had hurt them. Goody Bibber's accusing tongue stumbled, and she said, "He has not hurt me." Hobbs was appealed to, and he answered solemnly, "I can speak in the presence of God safely, as I may look to give account another day, that I am clear as a new-born babe."

The circle declared that he was even then going to this and that one, and torturing them, and Hathorne demands, "How can you be clear?" in view of what the children "saw." Then they fell into a fit and "hallooed."

Gossip is admitted to Court, and the Judge asks the prisoner when he was at any religious meeting.

"Not a pretty while."

"Why so?"

"Because I was not well. I had a distemper that none knows."

The Judge demands, "Can you act witchcraft here, and, by casting your eyes, turn folks into fits?"

"You may judge your pleasure. My soul is clear."

"Do you not see you hurt them by your look?"

"No, I do not know it."

"You did not answer to that question; don't you overlook them?"

"No, I don't overlook them."

"What do you call that way of looking upon persons and striking them down?"

"You may judge your pleasure."

"Well, but what do you call it?"

"It was none of I."

Then comes the ever ready, impertinent question of the Court, "Who was it then?" to which Hobbs gives the pertinent reply, "I cannot tell who they are." The Judge further urges against him what the circle "see" and feel of his hurtings, and demands, "Can you deny it?" to which the prisoner steadily answers, "I can deny it to my dying day."

The Judge then accuses him of going away when the Bible is read in his family. He flatly denies it. Good Deacon Ingersoll and Thomas Haynes come forward with a second-hand testimony, and say that Hobbs' daughter Abigail told them so. Thus new cords are added to the meshes that are being woven about William Hobbs, in bringing his family testimony against him, the testimony of a distracted, vagrant daughter, and an overawed and confounded wife. The Court pressed the advantage thus gained, and reminded him that the girls ceased to be afflicted by his wife and daughter when they began to confess.

"I am not guilty," is the justly defiant answer. The Judge, evidently piqued at his firmness, insults him by a perverted use of a sufficiently explained fact of his non-attendance for "a pretty while" upon religious service; at the same time charging his denial of guilt to the devil's influence over him. "If you put away God's ordinances from you, no wonder that the devil prevails with you to keep his counsel." He pushes for awhile the matter of the worship of God, without tripping the prisoner. He then comes back to his daughter. "Have you not known a good while that your daughter was a witch?"

"No sir."

"Do you think she is a witch now?"

"I do not know."

Failing in this, as in other demands, to extort any thing like a committal of the prisoner against himself, Hathorne resorts to a demand of the prisoner to explain the afflictions of the children. With unfaltering self-possession he answers that he does not know what ails them.

When it is remembered that William Hobbs had brought against him the confessions of his wife and daughter, and that the browbeating of the Court had not been exceeded in any other case, it will be allowed that he passed the examination with great excellence of temper, and a firmness of mind that could not well have been excelled. There was only "witchcraft evidence" against him, but with Hathorne that was good evidence, and Hobbs was sent to jail.

Mary Easty was sister to Rebecca Nurse and Sarah Cloyse—three excellent women, as we have stated, belonging to good families. Mary Easty was fifty-eight years old, and had seven children; her husband, Isaac Easty, owned and lived upon a large, well developed estate, and their religious and social relations were among the most favored as well as honorable. Her arrest, trial and commitment to prison have nothing peculiar in them to distinguish her case from that of others that have been given, except that she suffered with, and on account of, her loved sisters. She affirmed calmly and firmly her innocence, was browbeaten by the Court, (though much less than was William Hobbs,) was cried out against by the girls after this fashion: "O Goody Easty, O Goody Easty, you are the woman, you are the woman!" and was proved guilty of witchcraft by witchcraft evidence only.

The arrest, trial and commitment of Mary Black, an ignorant, negro slave of the Tituba type, shows that "the possessed" did not yet despise small game, though they shot at shining marks.

Philip English (arrested under a warrant obtained by Captain Jonathan Walcot, Mary's father, and Sergeant Thomas Putnam, the father of Ann) was a higher prize. He was one of the first "merchant princes" of the Massachusetts colony. He owned fourteen buildings in the town, a wharf, and twenty-one vessels. His business was extensive, and his social position of the very first class. His mansion in Salem, standing in the memory of many living, was spacious, constructed with taste, and charmingly located on the sea-shore. Jealousy of his affluence, and resentment on account of some lawsuits in which he had been engaged, are the surmised occasions of the accusations against him of witchcraft. His wife, also reputed of eminent character and culture, shared his arrest. Bentley says: "From the indulgence of her education she was not condescending to all the poor around her, and from them the accusations came. The officer came to her house in the evening of the 21st of April, 1692. The officer had been admitted by the servant, and read his warrant in her bed-chamber, but she refused to rise. Guards were placed around the house. In the morning she attended to the devotions of her family, kissed her children with great composure, proposed her plan of their education, took leave of them, and then told the officer she was ready to die. She was examined, and committed, by indulgence, to custody in a public house at which her husband visited her." The visits of Mr. English to his wife occasioned jealousy, of course, since accused members of families less wealthy, but not less innocent, were suffering in uncomfortable cells. In consequence, they were sent together to the "Arnold jail in Boston." There are no records of the trial which preceded their commitment. But the rich have friends. Two ministers of the First Church in Boston interposed their good offices in their behalf, and they escaped from jail. They immediately went to New York, carrying recommendations to the hospitality of the Governor, and there they remained until the collapse of the witchcraft *furor*, when they returned to their home in Salem. We have no such pleasant *finale* to relate of any others who were tried and committed for witchcraft.

Mrs. Susanna Martin, a widow of Amesbury,

was examined at the village meeting-house, May 2. She was a woman of an original character, and her trial has marked peculiarities. She is described as "a short, active woman, wearing a hood and scarf, plump and well-developed in her figure, and of remarkable personal beauty."

One accusation against her is singular. A woman of Newbury deposed that she walked from Amesbury to her house one "very dirty season," when the traveling was not fit for any one to be abroad. When she entered the room the children were bid make way for her to come to the fire to dry herself. Martin replied, "I am dry as you are." Her friend expressed a surprise that she did not seem to have wet the soles of her shoes. She cast aside her coat, and exclaimed, "I scorn to have a drabbled dress."

Mrs. Martin had fallen upon evil times indeed, when tidiness was made a presumption of witchcraft.

When before authority, this energetic woman showed that her scorn was not confined to a drabbled skirt. The accusing party presented their convulsions against her, Ann Putnam in a fit threw her glove at her, and "the examinant" laughed.

"Why do you laugh?" demands authority.

"Well I may at such folly."

"Is this folly, the hurt of these persons?"

"I never hurt man, woman, or child."

Mercy Lewis shouted that she hurt her and pulled her down, at which Martin laughs again. Others join in the outcry against her, and the Judge asks,

"What do you say to this?"

"I have no hand in witchcraft."

"What ails this people?"

"I do not know."

"But what do you think?"

"I do not desire to spend my judgment upon it."

"Do not you think they are bewitched?"

"No, I do not think they are."

"Tell me your thoughts about them."

"Why, my thoughts are my own when they are in; but when they are out they are another's."

"You said their master. Who do you think is their master?"

"If they be dealing in the black art, you may know as well as I."

"Well, what have you done toward this?"

"Nothing."

"Why, it is you or your appearance."

"I cannot help it."

"How comes your appearance just now to hurt these."

"How do I know?"

"Are not you willing to tell the truth?"

"I cannot tell; he that appeared in Samuel's shape, a glorified saint, can appear in any one's shape."

"Do you believe these do not say true?"

"They may lie, for aught I know."

"May not you lie?"

"I dare not tell a lie, though it may save my life."

"Then you will speak the truth?"

"I have spoken nothing else. I would do them any good."

Hathorne retorts that she had just insinuated that the children had the devil for their master, and he did not think therefore that she had great affection for them.

The marshal, who was standing by her, puts in a word, and the circle shout that they see her upon the beam. The Court and people no doubt gaze in vain in the direction toward which they point. Amid the hubbub the magistrate remarks solemnly, "Pray God discover you if you be guilty;" to which Mrs. Martin responds, "Amen! amen! A false tongue will never make a guilty person."

Mercy Lewis said tauntingly to the prisoner, "You have been a long time coming to the court to-day. You can come fast enough in the night."

"No, sweetheart," said Mrs. Martin, and then the circle performed generally. John Indian did the ground tumbling as he cried out, "She bites! she bites!" It was observed that at the same time Martin was biting her lips.

"Have you not compassion for these afflicted?" inquired Hathorne.

"No, I have none."

Several cried out just here that they saw the Black Man with her. The circle made an attempt to approach Mrs. Martin, but were not able. John Indian was plucky in the matter, and stalked toward her shouting, "I'll kill her." But he was flung to the floor before he reached her. Hathorne, as usual, holds the prisoner responsible for an explanation of these amazing phenomena, and demands why it is they cannot come near her. She answers, "I cannot tell. It may be the devil bears me more malice than another."

"Do you not see God is discovering you?" triumphantly exclaims Hathorne.

Nothing daunted, Martin replies, "No, not a bit for that."

"All the congregation think so."

"Let them think what they will."

"What is the reason these cannot come near you?"

"I do not know but they can if they will; or else, if you please, I will come to them."

The circle cry out that the Black Man is whispering in her ear, and Hathorne inquires what he says. She answers, "There was no one whispered to me." The words of the prisoner were "fiercer" than those of the Judge, but with the Court there was power, and she was consigned to prison.

The circle had grown bolder and keener in their manner of accusing, and they were now prepared to strike even "a reverend Elder."

CHAPTER XIV.

A Reverend Elder.

ON the evening of April 20, 1692, Ann Putnam had most fearful revelations and tortures at her home, in the presence of her father, Sergeant Thomas Putnam. The specter of a minister appeared to her, at which she was terribly affrighted. Dark insinuations had been made before by the circle of a man dressed in black at Casco, and other places in Maine had been referred to. Now the sea-coast of that far-off region sends fearful ghosts. Ann cries, "O, dreadful! dreadful! here is a minister come! What! are ministers witches too? Whence came you, and what is your name? for I will complain of you, though you be a minister, if you be a wizard."

Then the specter offers the book, and tells Ann to write in it, to which she replies, "I will not, though you tear me to pieces." She immediately receives awful tortures and rackings. But she persists in her refusal, and preaches the recreant minister a sermon: "Is it not dreadful that you, a minister, who should teach children the fear of the Lord, should come to persuade poor souls to give their souls to the devil!" She then breaks out into vehement expostulation: "O, dreadful!

dreadful! tell me your name that I may know who you are?" After more tortures the specter tells his name—the Rev. George Burroughs. The reader will recognize it as that of the pastor of Salem Village who fared so hard at the hands of the parish, especially at the hands of Lieutenant John Putnam. He had been for some years pursuing his quiet course as the laborious, self-sacrificing pastor of a small flock in Maine. Now, if Ann's witchcraft testimony is reliable, he has come to the village to ruin innocent children. He is a *stupid* wizard, if any at all, for he not only tells his name while on his diabolical errand, but assures Ann that he bewitched his two first wives to death, and that he murdered Mrs. Lawson and her child, put troops of soldiers to death in Maine, and made Abigail Hobbs and other village people witches.

Ann's sufferings during this fight with Burroughs were immense. Her father sat down the next day and wrote to their worships, John Hathorne and Jonathan Corwin, then at Salem, stating nothing definitely, but, after thanking them for their great and good work in the Village thus far, hinting at things "high and dreadful, a wheel within a wheel, at which our ears do tingle." This hint, he says, is to prepare them to be still further "a terror to evil doers and a praise to them that do well."

On the day this note was written, at eleven o'clock A. M., Benjamin Hutchinson and Abigail Williams were concerned in "an amazing" occurrence. They met in the road. Abigail told Benjamin that she had seen "a little black minister" who lived in Casco, Maine, and went on otherwise to describe Mr. Burroughs. She said he was a wizard, and told stories of his wonderful feats of strength. "Why," exclaimed Abigail, "there he is now!"

"Where?" inquires Benjamin in amazement. "Why, there," pointing to a rut of a cart wheel in the road. Benjamin had an iron fork in his hand, and he valiantly attacked the specter, though *he* saw nothing. The girl went into a fit, exclaiming, "You have torn his coat, for I heard it tear."

"Whereabouts?" shouted Benjamin. "On one side," is the reply.

The parties now go into Deacon Ingersoll's great room. The girl shouts again, "There he stands!" "Where? where?" cries Benjamin, drawing his rapier.

"He is gone, but there is a gray cat!"

"Whereabouts?"

"There! there!" pointing at the place. Benjamin struck at and killed the cat on the spot. To be sure, *he* did not see any thing; but Abigail assured him it was so, and that Sarah Good carried away the dead cat.

The same day after lecture these two persons, with Mary Walcot and Eleazer Putnam, were in Deacon Ingersoll's chamber. The deacon's latch-string was always out. The girls said that the room was full of witches in their apparitions. The young men made fight with their rapiers, and killed "a great black woman of Stonington and an Indian who came with her."

The blood streamed upon the floor, invisible of course to the valiant knights of the rapier. The girls rushed to a window, declaring that they saw a great company of witches on a hill, and that three of them lay dead there—the two slaughtered in the room and another whom they did not know.

Sergeant Putnam and others, under oath, made due report to the Court of the Rev. Mr. Burroughs' treatment of his daughter, testifying in full to her "hellish temptations and loud outcries;" and the other weighty matters we have just related were faithfully brought to the official notice of their worships.

But the conduct of Mr. Burroughs received further exposure. The visions of Ann Putnam were growing sublimely awful. The bolts which she launched at the head of the little dark-complexioned minister of Casco, were like fiery flashes from a black, sulphurous cloud. Her truly devout uncle, Deacon Edward Putnam, and her father, testify to the following facts as seen and felt by her in their presence, a little later than those already related: George Burroughs came and urged her to write in his book, which was refused. He then told her that his two deceased wives would soon come to her with their tongues full of lies which she should not believe. The two women did then immediately appear in winding-sheets and napkins about their heads. They turned their faces toward Burroughs, looking red and angry, charging him with cruelty, and declaring that their blood cried for vengeance against him. They further declared to him that they should be clothed with white robes in heaven, while he should be cast into hell. At this fearful denunciation Burroughs vanished. The murdered women then turned toward Ann, "looking as pale as a white wall." They then told her they were Burroughs' wives whom he had murdered, one of them removing her winding-sheet and showing where he had stabbed her to death under the left arm, covering the wound with sealing-wax. This, she said, was done in the Village parsonage. The other testified that she had been killed by Burroughs, assisted by his present wife, "because they would have each other." They charged Ann to tell these things in Court to Burroughs' face, threatening to appear there themselves if he did not own them.

These retiring, the Rev. Deodat Lawson's wife and daughter came, charging their death upon the same reverend Elder, followed by Goodman Fuller's wife, with a like charge in reference to herself.

From the point of view of the people of Salem Village, and of the magistrates, the guilt of the Elder was immense. People held their breath in consternation. The authorities were alert. The foe must be taken by surprise, or he would escape into the forest which surrounded his far-off home. Nothing must be done in Salem or the alarm would reach him. Some one slipped off to Boston, a warrant was obtained from a magistrate of that place and sent to the sheriff of the district in which the little minister lived. Strange that one who visited the Village so audaciously should have known its secrets so little! Field-marshal Partridge of Portsmouth surprised him in the midst of his family at his frugal meal; so says tradition. Up to this time the good man had known nothing of the crimes charged against him. Humbly, peacefully shepherding his flock in the wilderness, he little thought to see the fierce lions into whose jaws he so suddenly fell. Tradition further says that he was roughly hurried away without a moment's farewell parting or conference with his family. But we need not believe more against the authorities than the records declare. The warrant was dated in Boston, April 30; Partridge delivered Burroughs to the Salem jailer, May 4. The distance from Salem was one hundred miles. The journey was made, no doubt, on horseback, and over the rough roads of a new country. There was the caution and fiery energy, in the arrest, of an attack by the same men on a camp of Indian foes. And, in fact, they sincerely believed that a foe, more to be dreaded than savages, and more to be hated than French or Dutch, was combining his forces against Salem, and that George Burroughs was confederate with him.

As the fall of a minister into this great sin was one of the things "great and high, at which the ears did tingle"—"a wheel within a wheel"—his trial required a Court of special dignity. The Lieutenant-Governor, William Stoughton, and Samuel Sewall, came to Salem and sat on the bench with Hathorne and Corwin; Stoughton presided.

Burroughs was first brought before the ministry and judges only. They inquired concerning his partaking of the Lord's Supper, he being a member of the Church in Roxbury, and asked whether his children had been baptized. He acknowledged not having received the Supper at all times when he might, and that only his eldest child was baptized. What this had to do with the crime for which he was indicted we cannot see, except the inquiring parties considered the neglect of any Christian duty the sin of witchcraft; if so, the sin of witchcraft has continued to be prevalent unto this day.

When brought to the room of public examination the prisoner "knocked down" the members of the circle, who were now behind him, and tortured them generally; not, of course, touching them, he being guarded, if not strongly chained. Susanna Shelden testified to a visit from the prisoner's two deceased wives, who appeared to her as to Ann Putnam in their winding-sheets, accusing their husband of murdering them. On hearing this dreadful charge the cries, agonies, and tumblings of the whole company of the afflicted were so great, so protracted, and so deeply afflicting to the Court and people, that they were removed for awhile from the room. The prisoner was then asked what he thought of these things. He meekly replied, "It is an amazing and humbling providence, but I understand nothing of it."

In the absence of the girls, evidence was presented that Mr. Burroughs had exercised, as it was alleged, supernatural strength. As it has been stated, he was a short man, but seems to have had a compact, strong physical frame, systematically developed by gymnastic exercise while a student in Cambridge College, and made powerful by a frontier life. Some of the things said to be done by him he denied, and qualified the statements concerning others.

When the accused and accusers were again face to face, Mary Warren came forward with another kind of proof of his wizard character. She swore that Mr. Burroughs had a trumpet which he blew to summon the witches to their convocations. Its notes called them to the diabolical sacraments in Mr. Parris' orchard near the parsonage. Its capacity was truly wonderful, or witch ears were amazing quick to take in far distant sounds, for its blasts reached every forest and sea-girt settlement.

The "confessing" Abigail Hobbs added her echo of what others had said of him—that he was a conspicuous figure at the witch meetings near Mr. Parris' house.

In these testimonies of the girls against the prisoner they suffered much at his hands, or, rather, at the hands of his "appearance," in chokings and strangulations.

We will follow him to his lonely cell with our sympathy until we meet him again, when our deeper sympathy will be awakened.

The Jacobs House.

CHAPTER XV.

The Jacobs Family.

WE have introduced among our portraits George Jacobs, Sen., an old man with white, thin hair flowing down his neck and shoulders. A tall man, making a commanding figure in the days of his vigorous manhood, he now bends upon two crutches. Though infirm in body, we shall see that he has no craven spirit. He could meet a sharp accusation with a square answer. He was not afraid of the face of authority, and he laughed at the witchcraft evidence brought against him. Vain levity, though prompted by assured innocence before ludicrous accusations!

The Court commences the examination with the statement: "Here are them which accuse you of acts of witchcraft."

"Well, let us hear who are they, and what are they."

Abigail Williams comes forward with testimony after the circle fashion. The old man laughs. Turning to the Court to excuse his levity, he says, "Because I am falsely accused. Your worships, all of you, do you think this is true?"

"Nay, what do you think?" demands the Court.

"I never did it."

The old, profound, confounding question is ever upon the lips of the magistrate: "Who did it?"

"Don't ask me," is the pertinent answer, though his worship seems to think it impertinent, for he replies, "Why should we not ask you? Sarah Churchill accuseth you. There she is."

Sarah Churchill was a servant-girl, living in the family of Jacobs. We shall have occasion to note the drift of her testimony. It breathes a vindictive spirit.

Jacobs replies to Sarah's accusations, "I am as innocent as the child born to-night." He thinks to make a presumption of innocence out of a life of integrity, and adds an appeal to the Court, "I have lived thirty-three years here in Salem."

"What then?" replies the Court.

"If you can prove that I am guilty I will lie under it," persists the prisoner.

Here Sarah Churchill puts in the assertion that he came with two crutches to Deacon Ingersoll's the previous evening and afflicted her.

"Pray, do not accuse me. I am as clear as your worships. You must do right judgment."

Seeming not to hear this solemn appeal, the magistrate turns to the servant-girl and demands, "What book did he bring you, Sarah?"

"The same that the other women brought."

"The devil can go in any shape," interposes the old man.

"Did he not appear on the other side of the river and hurt you? did not you see him?" are the leading questions of the Court. "Yes, he did," is the accommodating reply.

The Judge turns with an air of triumph to the prisoner and says, "Look, then; she accuseth you to your face. She chargeth you that you hurt her twice."

"It is not true. What would you have me say? I never wronged no man in word nor deed."

"Here are three evidences."

"You tax me for a wizard. You may as well tax me for a buzzard. I have done no harm."

His worship assumes the point in question, which is never any question with him, and says, "Is it no harm to afflict these?"

"I never did it," is the prompt denial.

"But how comes it to be your appearance?"

"The devil can take any likeness."

The reader will note the answer of the Court, as it affirms the doctrine of the magistrates, as practically maintained throughout the trial, as distinguished from those of the ministers, as we shall have occasion more fully to understand—"Not without their consent." That is, the specter of a person assumed by the devil was, by this doctrine, a proof of the person's confederacy with him.

Jacobs replies, "Please your worship, it is untrue. I never showed the book. I am silly about these things as the child born last night."

The magistrates seem suddenly to call to mind the remark of Jacobs at the commencement of the examination, in which he says, "I have lived thirty-three years in Salem," implying a challenge to find a stain upon his character. His honor replies, "That is your saying. You argue you have lived so long. But what then? Cain might have lived long before he killed Abel; and you might have lived long before the devil had so prevailed on you."

Sarah Churchill interposes, saying, "I know you have lived a wicked life."

"Let her make it out," replies her master.

"Doth he pray in his family?" inquires the Court.

"Not unless by himself."

"Why do you not pray in your family?"

"I cannot read."

"Well, but you may pray for all that. Can you say the Lord's Prayer? Let us hear you."

It will be borne in mind that it was alleged in the witchcraft doctrine that a witch could not repeat the Lord's Prayer correctly. So they were put to this test in their examinations. In this case, say the records, 'He could not repeat it right after many trials."

The Judge asks Sarah Churchill if she was not frightened when the likeness of her master came to her. She answers, "Yes."

The prisoner seeing that every thing with which he was accused was assumed as true, exclaims resolutely, "Well, burn me or hang me! I will stand in the truth of Christ. I know nothing of it."

The magistrate inquires, "Do you know nothing of getting your son George and his daughter Margaret to sign?"

"No, nothing at all."

At the second examination of George Jacobs a day later, namely, May 11, the circle were exceedingly clamorous. Mary Walcot affirmed that he came and beat her with one of his crutches "to make her sign." Ann Putnam declared that he had told her that he had been a witch forty years. Of course she meant that his "appearance" told her so. This same wicked appearance stuck pins into the hands of Ann Putnam and Abigail Williams.

John Doitch, a boy sixteen years of age, appears on the stage only at this time. He came forward as one deeply afflicted by "old Jacobs" and others. His accusation is a very curious one. He says that "John Small and his wife Anne, both deceased and formerly of the town of Salem, did both appear to this deponent, and told him that they would tear him to pieces if he did not go and declare unto Mr. Hathorne that George Jacobs did kill them."

We presume, though the records are silent, that George Jacobs made answer to this impeachment, "I never did it." But as his specter was believed to have done the mischief, his answer availed nothing. Certainly his "appearance" should have been arrested, if any one; but the Court sent the veritable George Jacobs, Sen., to jail, to await, in irons, his trial.

The examination above narrated took place in the house of Thomas Beadle in Salem. Like Deacon Ingersoll at the Village, he kept an inn.

Why the Church was not used does not appear. It seems to show an abatement of popular feeling, but the subsequent trials do not sustain this view. Perhaps no special interest was felt in the plain old man.

His grand-daughter, Margaret, was examined and committed at the same time. There is no account of her trial, but we shall meet her on another occasion.

A few days after the trial of Margaret a warrant was taken out against her father, George Jacobs, Jun., and his friend and neighbor, Daniel Andrew. Andrew had been representative to the General Court, and a teacher of his neighbor's children in the essential branches of education in the absence of a regular teacher. He was a man of wealth, education, and piety. Jacobs, Jun., and Andrew, seeing that to be accused was to be judged guilty and imprisoned, and probably, in the final result, hanged, hastily left the Village, and escaped across the sea. A hard necessity, but wisely improved.

Rebecca Jacobs, wife of George Jacobs, Jun., was a truly unfortunate woman. She had been, for twelve years, known as one partially bereft of reason. But none were too high nor too low for the shafts of the "possessed" girls. They had caused the imprisonment of her daughter and father-in-law, and had driven her husband suddenly to a foreign land, without time to provide for the comfort or even the necessities of his family. The constable now came for her. She became desperate and showed fight. But she yielded on a promise of speedy release, which promise was not kept. Four children, one of them an infant, were left in her truly desolate home. Those who were old enough to walk followed their mother, crying and vainly endeavoring to overtake the officer. Compassion had not all failed for the families of the accused, and the neighbors took the little ones to their homes. The mother was committed to jail. Few families felt the desolating storm of witchcraft more than the Jacobs family.

CHAPTER XVI.

Curious, but Sad.

BRAY WILKINS was a yeoman of the olden time and of the purest type. He lived at "Will's Hill," on the boundary line between Reading and Salem, about five miles from the Village. He was an old man in 1692. He had owned a lordly extent of land, on which were located his own farm and those of his children. His present domain was ample, and was to him all the more valuable as it had become his by enterprise, skillful management, and unflinching persistence in hard work. Like Francis Nurse, he had bought this valuable estate, thirty-one years before, without capital—having only a ton of bar iron and twenty shillings at the time—had put his brains and strong hands against the mortgage, and it became his. He, his children and children's children, as the generations came on, plodded punctually over the long distance to the Village meeting-house to hear the word preached, and to secure thereby a better treasure in heaven.

Sadly, though not so destructively as with many, did the witchcraft movement break in upon the quiet of his old age.

Bray's grandson, John Willard, had been employed as a deputy constable, and been engaged in arresting the accused persons. He seems to have been a straightforward man of strong sense. He had seen much of the accusers, the accused, and their worships, the magistrates, and came to the conclusion that the accused were those deserving sympathy, and that the others were "bewitched." This he made free to express. At a friend's house, in familiar talk, he had exclaimed, "Hang them, they are all witches!" This of course was dangerous talk in those times. Whisperings against him began to fill the air. Hearing of these, he went one day to his grandfather's in much trouble, desiring of him and some neighbors, their counsel and prayers. The old man did not respond in a very Christian-like spirit, and seems to have had afterward, in relation to the request, a sore conscience. He put Willard off by saying that he was going from home, but if he returned before night he "should not be unwilling" to unite with others in prayers for him. But he came home late, and confesses that the prayers were not offered. Willard did not complain, but Wilkins said to the Court subsequently: "Whether my not answering his desire did not offend him, I cannot tell; but I was jealous, afterward, that it did."

The old man's jealousy, as it generally happens with that dangerous feeling, grew apace. Through it he saw an evil intent in every act and look of his grandson. The cords of family and neighborly confidence felt the strain of the witchcraft storm, and throughout the Village and town, and to some extent in all towns bordering on them, were snapping asunder.

Bray Wilkins about this time, it being election week, mounted his horse, took his wife on a pillion behind, and started for Boston. A brave old couple were they to ride this distance, over new roads, at fourscore years each! But election day was a "high day," and were they not yet young?

John Willard was minded also to go to election, having engaged the company of Henry Wilkins, Jun. Henry's son Daniel, seventeen years old, begged his father not to go, repeating the stories against Willard, and exclaiming, "It were well if John Willard were hanged!"

On election day our aged friend, nothing esteeming the weariness of the recent ride from Will's Hill, nor the excitement of the scenes just witnessed, rode out to Dorchester and dined with his brother, Lieutenant Richard Way. His former Pastor, Deodat Lawson, and his wife were there; all seems to have gone "as merry as a marriage bell" until Henry Wilkins and John Willard came in. There was perhaps soreness felt on the part of Willard; there was confessed jealousy on the part of Old Bray. He says, "To my apprehension, he looked after such a sort upon me as I never before discerned in any." Soon after the old gentleman was seized with severe pain, "like a man on a rack." He thus states the case: "I told my wife immediately that I was afraid that Willard had done me wrong; my pain continuing, and finding no relief, my jealousy continued. Mr. Lawson and others there were all amazed, and knew not what to do for me. There was a woman accounted skillful came hoping to help me, and after she had used means, she asked me whether none of those evil persons had done me damage. I said I could not say they had, but I was sore afraid they had. She answered, she did fear so too. As near as I remember, I lay in this case three or four days in Boston; afterward, with the jeopardy of my life, as I thought, I came home."

When he arrived at Will's Hill he found his grandson, Daniel Wilkins, who had warned his father not to go to election with Willard, in mortal agony. Increased consternation spread throughout the whole region. Who could be safe from the foe that thus walked in darkness and wasted at noonday! The Wilkinses generally began to have pains unimagined before. Parris and the circle rushed to the rescue. Mercy Lewis and Mary Walcot were invited to solve the mystery of the sufferings of the old man and his grandson! They stood by the bed of Daniel, seeing, as they declared, old Mrs. Buckley and John Willard "upon his throat and breast, pressing and choking him until the breath left his body, and he lay cold in death."

From this sad scene Mary Lewis went to the sick room of Bray. The friends asked her if she saw any thing. "I'm looking for John Willard," was the reply. Soon she exclaimed, "There he is upon his grandfather's belly!" The old man testified to the grievous pain "he did then feel in the small of his belly."

Mrs. Sergeant Thomas Putnam came to the help of the girls against Willard. There is surely now no hope in Willard's case! "A troop cometh" against him, shadowy, ghastly, and terrific. Mrs. Putnam sees them all, describes their appearance, and reports their testimony, every word of which is a shaft of fire to John. First comes Samuel Fuller and Lydia Wilkins in their winding-sheets, declaring to her that John Willard was their murderer. Then comes John himself, confessing the truth of the above charge, and adding the names of Goody Shaw, and Fuller's second wife, and Aaron Way's child, and Ben. Fuller's child, and Sarah, an infant child of Mrs. Putnam herself, and Philip Knight's child, (with the help of William Hobbs,) and Jonathan Knight's child, and two children of Ezekiel Cheever, (with the help also of Hobbs,) adding all these in his spectral confession to the list of those whom he had put to death. The appearance of Fuller and Wilkins threatened to tear Mrs. Putnam in pieces if she did not report their charge against the accused to Hathorne, and rather cautiously threatened to appear to the magistrates—"perhaps they would"—if they did not believe the accusation.

A coroner's jury, with Nathaniel Putnam as foreman, held their inquest over the body of young Daniel Wilkins. There is no direct account of its findings, but Bray, in a dispute with some persons concerning their belief that Willard was innocent, defends himself from responsibility for Willard's conviction by saying: "It was not I, nor my son Benjamin Wilkins, but the testimony of the afflicted persons, and the jury concerning the murder of my grandson, Dan Wilkins, that would take away his life if any thing did." So it may be inferred that the jury found Daniel's death to be caused by witchcraft through John Willard.

The warrant against Willard was taken the same day of the examination of Jacobs. But it was eight days before his apprehension. He fled, and all the marshals and their deputies in the colony were set on his track. He was arrested in Groton, and brought to Beadle's tavern in Salem, tried, and committed. He was, of course, condemned in fact long before.

We have no account of his examination. We can easily, and not unjustly to any parties, imagine the ghostly sights, and horrid tortures by him, of the girls, and the demand of Hathorne upon the prisoner to explain the phenomenon upon any other assumption than his confederacy with the devil, and his voluntary doing what his specter did.

Willard's case is curious, and some parts of it would be ludicrous were they not so sad in their results.

CHAPTER XVII.

The Christ-like Spirit.

MRS. ELIZABETH HOW was the wife of James How. They lived on the borders of Topsfield and Ipswich. We shall admire the Christian bearing of Mrs. How, and love her Christ-like spirit, which neither wrongs nor personal sufferings could overpower. Her husband, who was blind, will excite our sympathy. When we shall see, toward the close of the volume, the persistent devotion of their daughters to both parents in their sufferings, we shall greet them as our own sisters.

Though living away from the Village and town, the Hows evidently were conversant with good company, and with the means of improving mind and heart. Not so with at least some of their neighbors. They had not seen the school-master, nor do we think they often saw the meeting-house. Their complaints against Mrs. How as a witch are grounded upon circumstances that appear foolish even in comparison with those alleged elsewhere against other persons. An example or two will suffice to show this, and show the extreme demoralization of the people by the prevailing delusion.

Timothy Perley and wife had some time previous had "a difference" with Mrs. How about some boards. That very night the three cows of the Perleys lay out. In the morning they went to milk them, and, instead of the generous pailful they were wont to give, a meager quart or so was obtained. For several days this continued to be the milking, though "they were in a good English pasture;" then, "for no apparent reason, they returned to their old pailsful." Their inference was that Mrs. How had bewitched them, and with this matter the Court was entertained.

Another neighbor, Isaac Cummings, Sen., was applied to by Mrs. How's husband for the loan of a horse. Cummings happened not to be at home, and his son replied to the request that his father had only a mare, and he did not think he would like to lend it. This was Thursday. On Friday Cummings and his wife rode out on the mare, returning at night and turning her into the pasture "in good order to his thinking." In the morning she stood at his door, weary, worn in flesh, and bit sore. The usual remedies for ailing horses were applied, and one, at least, unusual one, we should think. A pipe of lighted tobacco was brought to the mare and immediately it blazed up, the flame covering the buttocks of the horse, and shooting up into the roof of the barn, which "crackled" with a noise heard outside as well as within. No man seemed to be the worse for the fire, but the conviction was deepened that "an evil hand" was in the affair.

One more remedy was proposed, which was to

burn a portion of the mare's flesh; but she dropped suddenly dead.

The connection of Mrs. How with these occurrences was established by the neighbors by a stroke of Judge Hathorne's logic—if *she* did not do it, who or what did?

But a more serious accusation was made against Mrs. How by Timothy and Samuel Perley. They charged her with bewitching a daughter of the latter, a girl ten years old. The girl, according to their testimony, had the usual tortures, pinches, and pricks with pins, besides being "pulled into the fire and sorely burned, and thrown into the water," which rough treatment continued two or three years, ending only with her death. The connection with Mrs. How was established by the usual spectral appearances.

But this good woman was not without consistent, earnest friends—those who came forward in her defense against her accusers. They put the case of the afflicted child of Samuel Perley in a different light.

The Rev. Samuel Phillips, of Rowley, gave, in substance, the following testimony: Being desired by Samuel Perley, he visited his house, in company with Rev. Mr. Payson, also of Rowley, to see the afflicted child, Hannah. When they were in the house she had one of her fits, but did not mention Mrs. How. When the attack was over Mrs. How, who was present, went to the child, took her hand and asked her if she had ever done her any hurt. She replied cordially, "No, never; and if I did complain of you in my fits I knew not that I did so."

Mr. Phillips further testified upon oath, "That young Samuel Perley, brother to the afflicted girl, looked out of the window, (I and the afflicted girl being without doors together,) and said to his sister, 'Say Goodwife How is a witch—say she is a witch;' and the child spake not a word that way. But I looked up to the window where the child stood, and rebuked him for his boldness to stir up his sister to accuse the said Goodwife How; whereas she had cleared her from doing any hurt to his sister in both our hearing; and I added, 'No wonder the child in fits did mention Goodwife How when her nearest relations were so frequent in expressing their suspicions, in the child's hearing when she was out of her fit, that the said Goodwife How was an instrument of mischief to the child."

Mr. Payson gave a like testimony.

Other witnesses said, under oath: "We have often spoke to Goodwife How of some things that were reported of her that gave some suspicion of that she is now charged with; and she always professing her innocency, often desired our prayers to God for her, that God would keep her in his fear, and support her under her burden. We have often heard her speaking of those persons that raised those reports of her, and we never heard her speak badly of them for the same; but, in our hearing, hath often said that she desired God that he would sanctify that affliction, as well as others, for her spiritual good."

Simon Chapman and Mary his wife testify that "They have been acquainted with the wife of James How, Jun., as a neighbor, for this nine or ten years, that they have resided in the same house with her by the fortnight together, and that they never found any thing but what was good in her. They found at all times by her discourse that she was a woman of afflictions, and mourning for sin in herself and others; and when she met with any affliction she seemed to justify God and say that it was all better than she deserved, though it was by false accusations from men. She used to bless God that she got good by affliction, for it made her examine her own heart. We never heard her revile any person that hath accused her of witchcraft, but pitied them and said, 'I pray God forgive them, for they harm themselves more than me. Though I am a great sinner I am clear of that, and such kind of affliction doth but send me to examine my own heart, and I find God wonderfully supporting me and comforting me by his word and promises.'"

Other neighbors gave equally full and explicit testimony of her readiness truly to bless those that cursed her, to do good to them that hated her, and to pray for them that despitefully used her and persecuted her.

The declaration concerning her by her husband's father, ninety-four years old, is quite to the purpose: "He, living by her for thirty years, hath taken notice that she hath carried it well becoming her place, as a daughter, as a wife, in all relations (setting aside human infirmities) as a Christian; with respect to myself as a father, very dutifully; and as a wife to my son, very careful, loving, obedient, and kind; considering his want of eye-sight, tenderly leading him about by the hand. Desiring God may guide your honors, I rest yours to serve."

Mrs. How was brought into court May 31.

It is but just that these testimonies of the Pastors of her town, and of those who well knew her, should be remembered in connection with the bearing of the examining magistrate toward her, and the final disposition of her case by the Court. The Village girls appeared against her in the usual manner. The Court demands: "What say you to this charge? here are them which charge you with witchcraft."

"If it was the last moment I was to live, God knows I am innocent of any thing in this nature."

The girls were continually "knocked down" by a glance of her eye, and brought out of a fit by touching her. When they attempted to approach her they were prostrated as if by a violent shock of electricity.

The Justice asks Mrs. How, "What do you say to these things? they cannot come to you."

"Sir, I am not able to give account of it."

"Cannot you tell what keeps them off from your body?"

"I cannot tell. I know not what it is."

"That is strange, that you should do these things and not be able to tell how."

Thus, as always, the Court assumed that the

falling down, recovery, and tortures of the accusers were by the will of the accused, and undeniable testimony of their guilt.

Mrs. Elizabeth How followed the other committed persons, in irons, to her cell.

Mrs. Mary Bradbury, wife of Captain Thomas Bradbury, of Salisbury, was another woman of Christ-like spirit. She was now, 1692, seventy-five years of age. The years of her married life, at least, had been spent among the people who were now called to judge whether there could be "a presumption" from her past spirit and conduct that she had committed the greatest crime possible to human depravity.

Her husband had been for more than fifty years trusted by his fellow-citizens with almost every office in their gift requiring capacity and high moral character. Their social position is recognized in the manner in which his wife is addressed, not as "Goody" or "Goodwife," but uniformly as "Mrs." Bradbury. At the time of her arrest she was in feeble health.

We have first:

"The answer of Mary Bradbury to the charge of witchcraft, or familiarity with the devil.

"'I do plead "not guilty." I am wholly innocent of any such wickedness, through the goodness of God that hath kept me hitherto. I am the servant of Jesus Christ, and have given myself up to him as my only Lord and Saviour, and to the diligent attendance upon him in all his holy ordinances, in utter contempt and defiance of the devil and all his works, as horrid and detestable, and accordingly have endeavored to frame my life and conversation according to the rules of his holy word; and in that faith and practice resolve, by the help and assistance of God, to continue to my life's end.

"'For the truth of what I say, as to matter of practice, I humbly refer myself to my brethren and neighbors that know me, and unto the Searcher of all hearts, for the truth and uprightness of my heart therein, (human frailties and unavoidable infirmities excepted, of which I complain every day.)

"'MARY BRADBURY.'"

Her husband thus testifies:

"*July* 28, 1692.—Concerning my beloved wife, Mary Bradbury, this is what I have to say: We have been married fifty-five years, and she hath been a loving and faithful wife to me. Unto this day she hath been wonderful laborious, diligent, and industrious in her place and employment about bringing up of our family, (which have been eleven children of our own, and four grandchildren.) She was both prudent and provident, of a cheerful spirit, liberal and charitable. She being now very aged and weak, and grieved under her affliction, may not be able to speak much for herself, not being so free of speech as some others may be. I hope her life and conversation have been such amongst her neighbors as gives a better and more real testimony of her than can be expressed by words. Owned by me,

"THOMAS BRADBURY."

The Rev. James Allin made oath before a magistrate, that having been nine years in the ministry in Salisbury, he had never known any thing in Mrs. Bradbury unbecoming the gospel; that she was a constant attender upon the ministry of the Word and all the ordinances of the gospel; full of works of charity and mercy to the sick and poor.

Robert Pike, a man of prominence and distinction, who had known Mrs. Bradbury "upward of fifty years," and John Pike, both indorsed Mr. Allin's testimony. More than this, one hundred and seventeen of her neighbors, most of them heads of families, among whom were persons of the highest social and moral standing, gave, in substance, the same high character to the accused as did her husband and Pastor. They say, among other warm commendations, that they never knew or heard that she "ever had any difference or falling out with any of her neighbors, man, woman, or child," but that, hazarding her health, and confronting every danger, she had served the needy."

Set against this life record were a few testimonies made up of such stuff as the following:

"The deposition of Richard Carr, who testifieth and saith, that about thirteen years ago, presently after some difference to be between my honored father, George Carr, and Mrs. Bradbury, the prisoner at the bar, upon the Sabbath at noon, we were riding home by the house of Captain Thomas Bradbury, I saw Mrs. Bradbury go into her gate, turn the corner of, and immediately there darted out of her gate a blue boar, and darted at my father—at my father's horse's legs, which made her stumble; but I saw it no more. And my father said, 'Boys, what do you see?' We both answered, 'A blue boar.'"

Zerubbabel Endicott was living at George Carr's at the time, and testifies to the same thing. He adds that, when they answered, "A blue boar," Carr asked, "Whence came it?" They said, "Out of Mr. Bradbury's gate." "Then," said he, "I am glad you saw it as well as I."

It is worthy of remark that George Carr was the father of Mrs. Ann Putnam, who was from Salisbury.

As Mrs. Bradbury was sent to jail to await her trial, when the death penalty would hang over her head, we may presume, in reference to her examination, the usual spectral visions on the part of the circle, in which they are tormented by the prisoner, and the customary assumptions of the Court.

CHAPTER XVIII.

Statements of Personal Sufferers.

JONATHAN CARY lived in Charlestown. While rumors were rife against a Mrs. Cary, he and his wife visited Salem Village to ascertain whether she was really the person meant. But it will be of special interest to have Mr. Cary tell the story of what he saw and suffered, and the more so as it enables us to have an inside view of the parties at the trials:

"*May* 24.—I having heard, some days, that my wife was accused of witchcraft, being much disturbed at it, by advice went to Salem Village, to see if the afflicted knew her; we arrived there on the 24th of May. It happened to be a day appointed for examination. Accordingly, soon after our arrival, Mr. Hathorne, Mr. Corwin, etc., went to the meeting-house, the place appointed for that work. The minister began with prayer; and, having taken care to get a convenient place, I observed that the afflicted were two girls of about ten years old, and two or three others of about eighteen; one of the girls talked most, and could discern more than the rest.

"The prisoners were called in one by one, and as they came in were cried out at, etc. The prisoners were placed about seven or eight feet from the justices, and the accusers between the justices and them. The prisoners were commanded to stand right before the justices, with an officer appointed to hold each hand, lest they should therewith afflict them; and the prisoners' eyes must be constantly on the justices, for if they looked on the afflicted they would either fall into fits or cry out of being hurt by them. After an examination of the prisoners, who it was afflicted these girls, etc., they were put upon saying the Lord's Prayer as a trial of their guilt. After the afflicted seemed to be out of their fits, they would look steadfastly on some one person and frequently not speak, and then the justices said they were struck dumb, and after a little time would speak again; then the justices said to the accusers, 'Which of you will go and touch the prisoner at the bar?' Then the most courageous would adventure, but, before they had made three steps, would ordinarily fall down as in a fit. The justices ordered that they should be taken up and carried to the prisoner, that she might touch them; and as soon as they were touched by the accused the justices would say, 'They are well,' before I could discern any alteration, by which I observed that the justices understood the manner of it.

"Thus far I was only a spectator. My wife also was there part of the time, but no notice was taken of her by the afflicted, except once or twice they came to her and asked her name. But I, having an opportunity to discourse with Mr. Hale, (with whom I had formerly acquaintance,) I took his advice what I had best do, and desired of him that I might have an opportunity to speak with her that accused my wife, which he promised should be. I acquainted him that I reposed my trust in him. Accordingly, he came to me after the examination was over, and told me I had now an opportunity to speak with her said accuser, Abigail Williams, a girl eleven or twelve years old, but that we could not be in private at Mr. Parris' house, as he had promised me. We went, therefore, into the ale-house, where an Indian man attended me, who, it seems, was one of the afflicted. To him we gave some cider; he showed several scars that seemed as if they had been long there, and showed them as done by witchcraft, and acquainted us that his wife, who also was a slave, was imprisoned for witchcraft. And now, instead of one accuser, they all came in, and began to tumble down like swine; and then three women came in to attend them.

"We in the room were all at a stand to see who they would cry out of, but in a short time they cried out 'Cary;' and, immediately after, a warrant was sent from the justices to bring my wife before them, who was sitting in a chamber near by waiting for this.

"Being brought before the justices, her chief accusers were two girls. My wife declared before the justice that she never had any knowledge of them before that day. She was forced to stand with her arms stretched out.

"I requested that I might hold one of her hands, but it was denied me. Then she desired me to wipe the tears from her eyes and the sweat from her face, which I did. Then she desired she might lean herself on me, saying she should faint.

"Justice Hathorne replied she had strength enough to torment these persons, and she should have strength enough to stand. I speaking somewhat against their cruel proceedings, they commanded me to be silent or else I should be turned out of the room.

"The Indian before mentioned was brought in to be one of her accusers. Being come in, he now, when before the justices, fell down and tumbled about like a hog, but said nothing. The justices asked the girls who afflicted the Indian. They answered, 'she,' meaning my wife, and that she now lay upon him. The justices ordered her to touch him in order to his cure, but her head must be turned away, lest, instead of curing, she should make him worse by looking on him, her hand being guided to take hold of his; but the Indian took hold of her hand and pulled her down to the floor in a barbarous manner. Then his hand was taken off, and her hand put on his, and the cure was quickly wrought.

"I, being exceeding troubled at their inhuman proceedings, uttered a hasty speech, that God would take vengeance on them, and desired that God would deliver us out of the hands of unmerciful men. Then her *mittimus* was writ.

"I did with difficulty and charge obtain the

liberty of a room, but no beds in it. If there had been, I could have taken but little rest that night.

"She was committed to Boston prison, but I obtained a *habeas corpus*, to remove her to Cambridge prison, which is in our own county of Middlesex. Having been there one night, next morning the jailer put irons on her legs, (having received such a command;) the weight of them was about eight pounds. These irons and her other afflictions brought her into convulsion fits, so that I thought she would have died that night. I sent to entreat that the irons might be taken off. But all entreaties were in vain if it were to have saved her life, so that in this condition she must continue.

"The trials at Salem coming on, I went thither to see how things were managed. Finding that specter evidence was there received, and idle if not malicious stories against people's lives, I did easily perceive which way the rest would go; for the same evidence that served for one would serve for all the rest. I acquainted her with her danger, and if she were carried to Salem to be tried I feared she would never return. I did my utmost that she might have her trial in our own county, I with several others petitioning the judge for it, and were put in hopes of it. But I soon saw so much that I understood thereby it was not intended, which put me upon consulting the means of her escape, which, through the goodness of God, was effected. She got to Rhode Island, but soon found herself not safe when there by reason of the pursuit after her. From thence she went to New York, along with some others that had escaped their cruel hands, where we found his excellency, Benjamin Fletcher, Esq., Governor, who was very courteous to us. After this some of my goods were seized in a friend's hands, with whom I had left them, and myself imprisoned by the Sheriff, and kept in custody half a day and then dismissed. But to speak of their usage of the prisoners, and the inhumanity shown to them at the time of their execution, no sober Christian could bear. They had also trials of cruel mockings, which is the more considering what a people for religion, I mean the profession of it, we have been; those that suffered being many of them Church members, and most of them unspotted in their conversation till their adversary the devil took up this method for accusing them. JONATHAN CARY."

The escape of Mrs. Cary from the snare of these witchcraft fowlers was plainly owing, "through the goodness of God," to the fearless energy of her husband. It is plain that he was neither deceived by the spectral theory of their worships, nor intimidated by their tyranny.

There is a curious sequel to this Cary affair. The woman cried out against by the girls was Elizabeth, wife of Captain Nathaniel Cary of Charlestown. The girls had seen her "appearance" —of course, her exact likeness, as they claimed—tormenting them. Jonathan and his wife, catching at the name of "Cary," as rumor published it, in the simplicity of their innocence, went to Salem Village, where they were unknown except to Mr. Hale. The girls, seeing the strangers, inquired their names, and, learning that it was Cary, from Charlestown, thought they had caught the one whom they had been accusing. It would seem, then, that spectral photographs did not enable the girls to determine living originals—a vital point concerning the value of their testimony. The warrant for Mrs. Hannah Cary's arrest read "Elizabeth, wife of Captain Nathaniel Cary," but in the hurry and confusion none noticed the error. The accusers, thinking that their originally intended victim had been dealt with, never further cried out against Elizabeth, who thus made an easy escape.

We have further the statement, from his own pen, of one who himself had been caught in the same snare—Captain John Alden. He had been commander of the colony's armed vessel; he had seen service in the French and Indian wars; had been a commissioner in conducting treaties with the Indian tribes, and was largely experienced as a sailor and naval commander—a tried and trusted man, of large property and good standing as a member of the Church. Captain Alden was a son of that Pilgrim of the Pilgrims, John Alden of the Mayflower, who had been dead now but six years. The Captain was seventy years of age in 1692, and so was born and cradled in that period of the Plymouth colony when its fathers were struggling to maintain its existence. He seems to have been a worthy son of this purest Puritanism.

How the Captain came to be "cried out against" by the circle is not known. He had lived in Boston thirty years, and was undoubtedly compromised by some informer coming between them.

"An account how John Alden, Sen., was dealt with at Salem Village.

"John Alden, Sen., of Boston, in the county of Suffolk, mariner, on the twenty-eighth day of May, 1692, was sent for by the magistrates of Salem, in the county of Essex, upon the accusation of a company of poor distracted or possessed creatures or witches; and, being sent by Mr. Stoughton, arrived there on the 31st of May, and appeared at Salem Village before Mr. Gedney, Mr. Hathorne, and Mr. Corwin.

"These witches being present who played their juggling tricks, falling down, crying out, and staring in people's faces, the magistrates demanded of them several times who it was, of all the people in the room, that hurt them. One of the accusers pointed several times at one Captain Hill, then present, but spake nothing. The same accuser had a man at her back to hold her up. He stooped down to her ear; then she cried out, 'Alden, Alden' afflicted her. One of the magistrates asked her if she had ever seen Alden. She answered, 'No.' He asked her how she knew it was Alden. She said the man told her so.

"Then all were ordered to go down into the street, where a ring was made; and the same accuser cried out, 'There stands Alden, a bold fellow, with his hat on before the Judges; he sells powder and shot to the Indians and French, and . . . has Indian papooses.' Then was Alden committed to the marshal's custody and his sword taken from him, for they said he afflicted them with his sword. After some hours Alden was sent for to the meeting-house in the Village, before the magistrates, who required Alden to stand upon a chair, to the open view of all the people, a good way distant from them. One of the magistrates bid the marshal to hold open Alden's hands, that he might not pinch those creatures. Alden asked them why they should think that he should come to that village to afflict those persons that he never knew or saw before. Mr. Gedney bid Alden to confess, and give glory to God. Alden said he hoped he should give glory to God, and hoped he should never gratify the devil, but appealed to all that ever knew him if they ever suspected him to be such a person, and challenged any one that could bring in any thing on their own knowledge that might give suspicion that he was such a one.

"Mr. Gedney said he had known Alden many years, and had been at sea with him, and always looked upon him as an honest man; but now he saw cause to alter his judgment.

"Alden answered he was sorry for that, but he hoped God would clear up his innocency that he would recall that judgment again; and added he hoped he should, with Job, maintain his integrity till he died.

"They bid Alden look upon the accusers, which he did, and then they fell down.

"Alden asked Mr. Gedney what reason there could be given why Alden's looking upon *him* did not strike *him* down as well; but no reason was given that I heard.

"The accusers were brought to Alden to touch them; and this touch, they said, made them whole.

"Alden began to speak of the providence of God in suffering these creatures to accuse innocent persons.

"Mr. Noyes asked Alden why he should offer to speak of the providence of God. 'God, by his providence,' said Mr. Noyes, 'governs the world and keeps it in peace,' and so went on with discourse, and stopped Alden's mouth as to that.

"Alden told Mr. Gedney that he could assure him there was a lying spirit in them; for I can assure you there is not a word of truth in all these say of me. But Alden was again committed to the marshal and his *mittimus* was written.

"To Boston Alden was carried by a constable; no bail would be taken for him, but was delivered to the prison keeper, where he remained fifteen weeks, and then, observing the manner of the trials, and the evidence then taken, was at length prevailed with to make his escape.

"Per John Alden."

CHAPTER XIX.

The Special Court.

WE have thus far noticed the cases of persons whose arrest and trial show the grounds of the proceedings of the Court, and the spirit of the accusers and prosecutors. We have omitted many, because the details are essentially the same as in those given. One feature running through all the trials, of great interest and significance, we shall give in the chapter on "confessions," illustrating it by curious facts.

The infatuation was now fearfully intense. We have but to notice one direction which it took, showing this fact, before we turn our attention to the Court which was intrusted with the fearful responsibility of the death penalty.

A man in Andover had a sick wife. We suppose the physicians had exhausted their skill upon her, and, being baffled by the disease, as the most skillful doctors will be, had given dark hints of an evil hand. At any rate the husband, in the simplicity of his heart and the darkness of his understanding, went to Salem Village and obtained two of the circle girls, and carried them to his home to reveal to him the mystery of his wife's illness. They fitly personated Pestilence and Death as they entered the town. They saw, of course, ghostly tormentors upon the person of the sick woman, and cried out against them. The flames of excitement were like a prairie fire driven by a fierce wind. In a short time after the visit of the girls, they had been the means of sending fifty persons to prison, to await in chains a threatened death on the gallows. To escape accusations, people turned accusers, and thus lied against the lives of neighbors and friends. A tempting refuge from the wrath of the storm was afforded by confession, and thus many, as we shall see, to save life imperiled their souls. Dudley Bradstreet, the magistrate of Andover, sat on the bench, listening to the witchcraft exhibitions and testimony, until he had committed forty to prison. His soul then sickened, his returning reason revolted at the proceedings, and he refused to sit in judgment on any others. This step proved that even magistrates were not beyond the reach of the Satanic accusations. He and his wife were seen in specter at the torturing business, and they had to flee for their lives. John Bradstreet, brother of this flying justice, was accused of "afflicting" a dog—a small business—and he too fled, while his disappointed prosecutors contented themselves with "executing" the dog. Why a poor brute should lose his life for being bewitched, and a bewitched girl be pitied, and invested with the fearful power of taking the lives of others, is not explained by the records.

While the panic at Andover was, at one time, equal perhaps in its fury to that of any place in the country, there was, as we shall see, a reactionary power there which was early and decidedly exerted.

Such had been the history of the witchcraft delusion, and such was its pending condition, as we have briefly described in the preceding pages, when a special commission was appointed by the Governor of the colony to hear and determine finally the witchcraft cases. It was known as the Court of Oyer and Terminer. Sir William Phipps, the Governor, had arrived at Boston from England on the 14th day of May. William Stoughton, of whom we shall know more, was now Lieutenant-Governor in the place of Danforth. Bartholomew Gedney, John Hathorne, Jonathan Corwin, Samuel Appleton, and Robert Pike, were in the Council from Essex County.

The new rulers did not interfere with the witchcraft proceedings, except that Mr. Gedney was sent to aid Hathorne and his associates, thus giving them "aid and comfort." Gedney presided at their sessions. Thus affairs stood when the special court was created by the Governor and his Council. It is an interesting fact that their right to appoint such a court has always been doubted by high authority. This power, it is believed, required the concurrence of the House of Representatives. Had the Governor and Council waited to convene this important branch of the government it would have carried the special court into the time when the reaction had set in, and its power would have been lost, and no lives sacrificed. Our history would then have been more of a comedy than a tragedy.

The justices constituting the Court were all members of the Council. Lieutenant-Governor William Stoughton was appointed Chief-Justice. His associates were John Richards, Wait Winthrop, Samuel Sewall, and Peter Sargent, all of Boston; Nathaniel Saltonstall of Haverhill, and Bartholomew Gedney of Salem. The Chief-Justice resided in Dorchester, so that only two of the Court were citizens of Essex County.

George Corwin, nephew of Jonathan Corwin who had been associated with Hathorne in the lower court, was appointed sheriff of the county, and Herrick acted as deputy. The title of "marshal" had ceased. Sheriff Corwin was only twenty-six years of age. He was son-in-law to one of the justices, and two others were his uncles. He needed, in the end, all these family influences to shield him from the vindictive feelings following the collapse of the delusion. His official duties, though less responsible than those of the judges, were even more painful.

The Court opened in Salem in the first week in June. The place of meeting was now the court-house, used also as a town-house. Thomas Newton of Boston had been commissioned to act as attorney-general.

The records of this Court are not in existence. What we know of its doings is learned from early writers. Hutchinson is believed to have had access to the records, as he gives dates and other details in some of the cases which he describes. Why these records have been taken from the files of court papers, where, no doubt, they once were, is not certainly known. It is natural to suppose that the immediate children of the chief actors in the painful transactions of the Court may have found means, in accordance with their wishes, to blot out, so far as these were concerned, their remembrance.

We are now prepared to meet again some of those whom we have followed to their dreary prisons.

CHAPTER XX.

A Fatal Result, and a Pause.

TWICE we have had Bridget Bishop before us in the shifting scenes of our story. We shall easily recognize her now, though seen under more solemn circumstances than before. As she is just from several weeks' confinement in a felon's cell, she must not be expected to appear in her "black cap and black hat, and red paragon bodice, bordered and looped with several colors." She has something more serious to think of than her "shovel-board." She cannot drive the circle girls from the Court as she drove from her premises the mean accusing man, who came calling for a pot of cider, with a spade wielded lustily in his retreating rear. Happy would it have been for all concerned if she had been intrusted with a scourge of cords, with power to expel by it, from their dishonored places, both Court and witnesses.

The first witness against her was her Pastor, Rev. Mr. Hale of Beverly. Several years before she had been accused of witchcraft by an insane, wretched woman, who in her lucid moments disowned her accusations; she had finally, overpowered by her mental disease, committed suicide. Mr. Hale then examined the case, and declared "Sister

Bishop" not deserving the suspicion of having by witchcraft murdered the woman. Now he reviews the whole matter under the misleadings of the prevalent infatuation, and renders under oath the following statement: "As to the wounds she died of, I observed three deadly ones; a piece of her windpipe cut out, and another wound above that through the windpipe and gullet, and the vein called jugular. So that I then judged and do now apprehend it impossible for her, with so short a pair of scissors, to mangle herself so without some extraordinary work of the devil or witchcraft."

When, many years before, Mrs. Bishop lived in the town of Salem, she had a neighbor by the name of Samuel Shattuck. Shattuck was a hatter, and Bridget carried to him articles of dress to be dyed, very likely, among others, the ribbons with which her "paragon bodice" was "looped." Her manners, in her frequent coming, were "smooth and flattering," in the estimation of the hatter, at least, after he began to suspect her of witchcraft. The eldest son of the hatter was, when Bridget began her calls, a healthy child, sound in body and mind. As her calls became frequent, his health commenced to decline. When standing in the door-way he would fall into a fit, and seemed to his parents "to be thrust out by an invisible hand," being cut and bruised thereby "in a miserable manner." When in his fits he gasped painfully for breath, his face and eyes at the same time dreadfully distorted. When not in his fits, he was continually moaning or crying piteously.

He was often falling either into the fire or water. Reason yielded under these bodily sufferings, and he became imbecile in mind.

In view of all these wonderful occurrences, which utterly confounded the doctors, the hatter and his wife "did think that he is bewitched; and did believe that the aforesaid Bridget Bishop is the cause of it."

John Cook, a neighbor's son, eighteen years of age, had the following remarkable experience: "About five or six years ago, one morning about sunrise, as I was abed, I saw Goodwife Bishop stand in the chamber by the window; and she looked on me, and grinned on me, and presently struck me on the side of the head, which did very much hurt me. Then I saw her go out under the end window at a little crevice about as big as I could thrust my hand into. I saw her again the same day, which was the Sabbath-day, about noon, walk across the room; and having, at the time, an apple in my hand, it flew out of my hand into my mother's lap, who sat six or eight feet distance from me; and then she disappeared." John's mother and several others were in the room, but they "affirmed they saw her not."

The next who take the stand are John Bly and his wife Rebecca. They had, at some time, a business transaction with Bridget, in which she sold John a hog. Now it occasionally happened in the days of our fathers, as in our days, that in the final settlement of such transactions one or both the parties were afflicted. But in this case it was the hog, as witnesses did swear, which was "afflicted." "She was taken with strange fits, jumping up and knocking her head against the fence, and seemed blind and deaf. She refused to suckle her pigs and foamed at the mouth." Being advised by a sensible neighbor, they gave the sow ochre and milk, upon taking which she was for awhile well. But she ran mad again, getting into the street and so running and jumping as to frighten John and his wife, and people generally, but, having had her run and jump, "was well again." The conclusion of the testimony runs thus: "We," said Bly and wife, "did then apprehend or judge, and do still, that said Bishop had bewitched said sow."

William Stacey takes the stand and testifies that as he was "once on a time a-going to mill" he met Bridget Bishop. After some conversation they parted. "Then," says Stacey, "being gone about six rods from her, said Bishop, with a small load in his cart, suddenly the off-wheel slumped or sunk down on plain ground; that this deponent was forced to get some one to help him get the wheel out. Afterward this deponent went back to look for said hole where his wheel sunk in, but could not find any hole."

Stacey had miserable luck when he met Bridget. He was, as he testified, passing, at another time, a brick kiln, when he met said Bishop. He had on a small load. The ground, just after passing her, was slightly ascending. But up the hill Stacey's horse could not budge. When he attempted to do so, under his master's promptings, "all his gear and tackling flew to pieces, and the cart fell down."

Stacey adds, "This deponent hath met with several other of her pranks at several times, which would take up great time to tell of."

But he takes time to make the most serious charge of all. He says, in conclusion, though very vaguely for so grave a matter: "This deponent doth verily believe that said Bridget Bishop was instrumental to his daughter Priscilla's death. About two years ago the child was a likely thriving child, and suddenly screeched out, and so continued in an unusual manner for about a fortnight, and so died in that lamentable manner."

John Louder was a servant of Gedney, one of the judges on the bench of the special court. He was a neighbor to Mrs. Bishop when she lived in town. The servant then quarreled with her about her fowls, which had trespassed upon his master's premises. Just after the quarrel he had an awful experience. He says, "I, going to bed about the dead of the night, felt a great weight upon my heart, and, awaking, looked, and, it being bright moonlight, did clearly see said Bridget Bishop, or her likeness, sitting upon my stomach; and putting my arms off of the bed to free myself from the great oppression, she presently laid hold of my throat and almost choked me, and I had no strength or power in my hands to resist or help myself; and in this condition she held me till almost day."

Some days after this, Louder, not being well,

remained at home on the Sabbath. Thus alone, the doors being shut, he "did see a black pig in the room coming toward him;" attempting to give it a vigorous kick "it vanished away."

It was very bad for Louder that he allowed a little illness to keep him from the house of God on the Sabbath, for only a short time after the black pig encounter he was at home again on that holy day. On this occasion a black thing jumped into the window and planted itself before his face. It had the body of a monkey, the feet of a cock, and the face of a man. John, in amazement and sore fright, sat trembling while the monster delivered its diabolical message. Among other flattering words it told him that if he would submit to its rule "he should want for nothing in this world." But Louder's resentment was aroused at this betraying of the cloven foot, and, doubling his fist in the monster's face, he exclaimed, "You devil, I'll kill you!" The vigorous blow from Louder which followed this threat sent the specter out of the window. But it returned to him in the porch, though the doors were shut, and received for its pains a fierce assault with a stick from the valorous servant. The stick was broken by the violence of its concussion with the door-sill, and John's arm "disenabled." But the foe was not quite vanquished, though made to retreat. It took its stand not far from the door, and when Louder came out, "seemed to be a-going to fly at him." But John was game. He cried out, "The whole armor of God be between me and you." This was too much for the monster. "It sprang back, and flew over the apple-tree, flinging the dirt with its feet against the witness' stomach, and shook many apples from the tree as it flew over."

The connection of all this with Bridget Bishop was established by the following very decisive evidence. As John went out of the porch, in following the specter, he "espied Bridget Bishop in her orchard going toward her house." He was, moreover, unable for the moment to take a step forward; and when he was struck by the dirt the specter threw against his stomach, he became dumb and remained so three days.

Such was some of the original evidence before this special court. The girls are known to have been there. There was nothing new in their acting, but they may be presumed to have become greater adepts in it. The confessors declared that she had been their accomplice. The new judges were not a whit behind their predecessors in credulity. They heard, wondered, believed, and condemned. Bridget Bishop went out of the court-room under the sentence of death. A week later she was hanged on Witch Hill.

The Court, having thus shown what might be expected of it, adjourned to the 30th of June. In the meantime the Governor and his council consulted the prominent ministers concerning the all-absorbing subject of witchcraft in Salem Village. This was an old practice under the colonial charter. "The several ministers consulted" returned answer, dated in Boston, June 15 1692. They express deep sympathy for "our poor neighbors that are now suffering by molestation from the invisible world." They are thankful for the success "a merciful God has given to the sedulous and assiduous endeavors of our honorable rulers to defeat the abominable witchcrafts," and pray that the good work may be perfected. They declare it as their judgment "that, in the prosecution of these and all such witchcrafts, there is need of a very critical and exquisite caution, lest by too much credulity for things received only upon the devil's authority there be a door opened for a long train of miserable consequences, and Satan get an advantage over us." They declare that all proceedings toward those that may be complained of "should be managed with exceeding tenderness, especially if they have been persons formerly of unblemished character." They disapproved of noise and openness in the examinations, and the admission of such tests against the suspected, "the lawfulness of which may be doubted by the people of God." "Evidence for committal, and, much more, for final condemnation," they say, "ought certainly to be more considerable than barely the accused person's being represented by a specter unto the afflicted; inasmuch as it is an undoubted and a notorious thing that a demon may, by God's permission, appear, even to ill purposes, in the shape of an innocent, yea, and a virtuous man. Nor can we esteem alterations made in the sufferers, by a look or a touch of the accused, to be an infallible evidence of guilt, but frequently liable to be abused by the devil's legerdemain." They suggest that possibly the devils may have taken a remarkable affront at their disbelief of testimony whose whole credit is from the devils alone, and that this affront may put an end to the dreadful calamity of so many persons being accused.

They close by saying, "Nevertheless, we cannot but humbly recommend unto the government the speedy and vigorous prosecution of such as have rendered themselves obnoxious, according to the directions given in the laws of God, and the wholesome statutes of the English nation, for the detection of witchcrafts."

The reader can but notice that the line of proceeding marked out as the one of wisdom and equity by the ministers was in many particulars the opposite of that which their "honorable rulers" had pursued, from the very first to the last of the witchcraft trials at Salem Village and Salem. Instead of "exquisite caution" there had been an apparent disregard of all caution. In the place of "exceeding tenderness" toward the accused, they had reserved all that kind of feeling for the accusers, even when the prisoners at the bar had been "persons formerly of an unblemished reputation." The openness of the trials had invited the noise and the exposure of the suspected which the ministers deprecated. The specter evidence and alterations made in the sufferers by the look and touch of the accused, by which, they declared, an innocent person might be condemned, had been the staple evidence in all the trials, and in most of them absolutely all that had been brought forward.

On what grounds, then, did the ministers see occasion for "thankfulness?" wherein was there proof that "success" had crowned the endeavors of the Court to detect witchcraft? If the evidence had not been legal a just conviction had failed. But we shall better understand this part of the letter of the ministers in the final development of our narrative.

CHAPTER XXI.

An Extorted Verdict.

THE Court met again on Wednesday, June 29th. They were in no wise improved by the intermission. The whole air was tainted by the delusion, and they were not proof against its infection, if indeed their presence among the people did not give it extension and intensity. In the short space of three weeks five more matrons had suffered the death penalty on Witch Hill. Of the circumstances attending the trial and execution of three of them, Sarah Wildes, Elizabeth How, and Susanna Martin, we know nothing. The reader will recollect the kind bearing of Mrs. How at her trial for commitment, her tenderness toward even her Satanic accusers, her patience with the unjust Judges, and her Christian spirit throughout. Even with the gallows before her eyes we feel assured that her faith triumphed, and that she prayed for her enemies, with her dying Master, "Father, forgive them, for they know not what they do."

We should not expect the same meekness from Susanna Martin. Her prayers were doubtless sincere and fervent, while at the same time her reproofs were just and cutting. Though she could not silence the Judges, nor evade their terrible power, they could not overawe her free and fearless spirit.

Of the poor, suffering, demented Sarah Good, in her arraignment for the death sentence, we know a little.

The afflicted acted against her as usual. One of them in coming out of a fit cried out in an agony that Good had cut her with a knife, and broken the blade in her flesh. Search was made, and a piece of the blade found on her person. Of this confirmation of her testimony the wondering and credulous Court was informed. But a young man in the crowd courageously stepped forward and exposed the fraud. He showed the handle and the remaining part of the blade to which the piece belonged. He declared that he had broken it only the day before, and thrown the piece away in the presence of the accusing girl. The Court dismissed the noble and brave boy, told the girl not to lie, and coolly continued to use her testimony against the lives of the prisoners.

Mr. Noyes, whom we have met before, one of the scribes of the Court, and minister of Salem, followed small game when he pressed this woman with his assumptions on her examination. "You are a witch, and you know you are a witch," was his insolent declaration. The outrage provoked from the suffering victim, standing on the verge of eternity, the unbecoming reply, "You are a liar; I am no more a witch than you are a wizard;

and if you take away my life, God will give you blood to drink."

We have endeavored, in the preceding pages, to make the reader well acquainted with the Nurse family. We have followed Francis Nurse and his wife Rebecca through their noble and successful enterprise of becoming the owners of the Townsend Bishop estate. We, at one time, saw them in their honored mansion, with their sons and daughters settled on farms in the vicinity—apparently an intelligent, united, Christian family connection. A foe as relentless as death, and incomparably more to be feared, entered the parental home, blasted the fair name of the wife and mother, immured her in a cell, and loaded her with chains. She now comes forth to stand before a blinded Court, diabolical witnesses, and a jury perverted, not only by the frenzied people without, but by the judges appointed to give them wise counsel. The path from the jail, *through the court*, led only to Gallows Hill.

We have spoken of the people as frenzied by the witchcraft storm, but before the pure character of this aged matron it had moments of partial cessation. Nathaniel Putnam, the second in years and now the oldest survivor of the three heads of the great Putnam family, dared to speak before Authority and a prejudiced crowd in her behalf. He testified that he had known her forty years, and that, "human frailties excepted, her life and conversation have been according to her profession; and she hath brought up a great family of children and educated them well, so that there is in some of them apparent savor of godliness."

This testimony of "Landlord Putnam" ought to have been the more influential, as he had, in their commencement, largely countenanced the witchcraft proceedings. It was the testimony of a man of wealth, advanced years, and of high standing in the Church and community at large.

Another paper was drawn up, of similar import, and signed by thirty-nine persons of the Village and vicinity, all of marked prominence and known excellence of character. It contained the name of Jonathan Putnam, a son of the Lieutenant John, one of the signers of the complaint against Rebecca Nurse which caused her arrest.

But the Court was deaf to these truthful words in behalf of the prisoner. They seemed to see only the sufferings of "the afflicted," and to hear only their wonderful ghostly stories.

There was one method of detecting a witch which the Court adopted after the teachings of the witchcraft theory, to which we have before alluded. It taught that witches had teats on some parts of their bodies, by which they suckled their imps, thus imparting to them their own diabolical venom. A jury of the sex of the suspected person, attended by a surgeon, were appointed to search the nude body for these teats. It generally happened that their excited imaginations saw them in any hardened portion of the flesh which might protrude above the rest, or in any deformity resulting from sickness or age. The records frequently speak of these juries, and contain their returns. In George Jacob's case, such teat was found "within his mouth, upon the inside of his right cheek." A cunning hiding place! Of the many outrages in these trials against the suspected, these indecent searchings were not the least.

Just before being brought to trial, Rebecca Nurse was subjected to such examination by a jury of women, who, seeing with deluded eyes, found upon her the diabolical marks. Two days before the meeting of the Court, she addressed to the judges a touching remonstrance against this return of the female jurors. She states the fact that the most aged and skillful of their number dissented from their decision. She affirms that nothing can be found upon her person not common to women of her age and infirmities, and finally respectfully petitions for a new examination, suggesting the names, as a part of the jury, of several experienced and well-known midwives.

Her daughters, Mrs. Preston and Mrs. Tarbell, women who had long been heads of families, and of established good name, testify to their mother's freedom from the suspected marks.

But all these words, expressing convictions of the innocence of the accused, were uttered to adders' ears. The same ears were, however, very quick to hear the circle as they raved against her.

Mary Walcot and Abigail Williams charged her with having committed several murders. They named the deceased Benjamin Houlten, John Harwood, and Rebecca Shepard as among her victims;

her sister Cloyse, they affirmed, assisting in their murder.

Mr. Parris was an ever ready volunteer accuser. He testified that, a certain person being sick, Mercy Lewis was sent for. She was struck dumb on entering the sick chamber. She was bid hold up her hand if she saw any witch apparition upon the sick person. Presently she raises her hand and goes into a trance. Gradually she recovers her speech and begins to mutter, "Goody Nurse," and then "Goody Carrier." There they are, plainly visible to spectral eyes, grasping the head of the sick man.

Of course, Mrs. Ann Putnam and her daughter Ann came down upon the poor prisoner with their terrific array of specters. The mother equaled her best efforts in the earlier trials. She describes in a glowing manner the "hellish temptations" and "dreadful tortures" she had of late suffered and was then suffering at the hands and by the presence of Rebecca Nurse. The "red book" and "black pen" are flourished with good effect. Troops of murdered men, women, and children, ghastly pale and in winding-sheets, are introduced at the proper time. The "free grace and mercy" of "Almighty God," in delivering her "out of the paws of those roaring lions and jaws of those tearing bears," have a devout recognition.

Ann comes in and declares that the presence of Nurse at the fiendish business described by her mother was plainly seen by her. But Ann is no mere retailer in court of what others say or saw, as is her Pastor, Mr. Parris. She has a special list of testimony, a little out of the common beaten track, and has, concerning it, a good indorser. While Rebecca Nurse was lying in the Salem jail carefully chained, Ann, being at the same time in the Village, was bitten by said Nurse. Her testimony on the point is very specific—it was "two of the clock of the day after her committal." Nurse did at the same time strike her with her spectral chain, and, in the course of half an hour, gave her six blows. One of the blows was especially "remarkable." Deacon Edward Putnam, her uncle, testifies that he saw "the marks both of bite and chains."

John Tarbell, son-in-law of Mrs. Nurse, and Samuel Nurse her son, went to Mrs. Ann Putnam's, after the commitment of their mother, to cross-question her and the girls who might be there concerning the accusations against their mother. After much talk he was told that the girl said she saw the apparition of a pale-faced woman sitting in her mother's seat, but did not know her name.

"Who was it that told her that it was Goody Nurse?" inquires Tarbell.

"Mercy Lewis said it was Goody Nurse," says Mrs. Putnam.

"No, Goody Putnam said it," replies Mercy.

So they gave the lie to each other on this important point.

The results of this visit were sworn to in court by these competent and credible witnesses, but, of course, they could not shake the faith of their worships in such matter-of-fact witnesses as Mrs. Ann Putnam and her daughter.

Having thus profoundly considered the case, the Court give it to the jury. These twelve honest men, sworn to decide according to law and evidence, go out and weigh what has been said by their honors and the witnesses, and return a verdict of—"*Not guilty!*"

It was like a bomb-shell bursting in a sleeping camp. The possessed accusers were instantly on the rampage. Those in the court set up "a hideous outcry," and those outside responded in unison. The spectators were filled with "amazement," and the Court was "strangely surprised." "One of the judges expressed himself not satisfied; another of them, as he was going off the bench, said they would have her indicted anew."

But the Chief-Justice was master of the situation, coolly remarking amid the uproar that "he would not impose on the jury." *That* might be the last feather which would break the back of the patience of outraged justice; but he would intimate that "they had not well considered one expression of the prisoner when she was upon trial, namely, that when one Hobbs, who had confessed herself to be a witch, was brought into court to witness against her, the prisoner, turning her head to her, said, 'What! do you bring her? She is one of us,' or words to that effect."

The "intimations" of the Chief-Justice, thus expressed, the murmurings of his colleagues on the bench, the threat of a new trial by one of them, the outcries of the bewitched, and the dissatisfaction of the crowd, prevailed. The jury went out to reconsider their verdict. But even now, under this enforced reconsideration, the case seems to have hung for some time in even scales in the minds of the jury. Their foreman, Thomas Fisk, being desired a few days after the trial, by some of the relatives, "to give a reason why the jury brought her in *guilty* after the verdict *not guilty*," gave the following explanation: "After the honored Court had manifested their dissatisfaction of the verdict, several of the jury declared themselves desirous to go out again, and thereupon the Court gave leave; but when we came to consider the case, I could not tell how to take her words as an evidence against her until she had a further opportunity to put her sense upon them, if she would take it."

This was certainly sensible and just in the foreman to wish Mrs. Nurse to have an opportunity "to put her sense upon" the words which the Chief-Justice had seized to crowd the fatal verdict upon her. He returned, as he states, to the court-room and asks for such an explanation, the prisoner sitting at the bar; he adds, "she being then at the bar, but made no reply nor interpretation of them; whereof these words were to me a principal evidence against her."

Fatal silence! But why did not the prisoner give the desired explanation? She shall answer for herself. When told, after the verdict and death sentence, what use had been made of her words, she put in the following declaration: "These presents to humbly show to the honored Court and jury that I being informed that the jury brought me in guilty upon my saying that Goodwife Hobbs and her daughter were of our company; but I intended no otherwise than that as they were prisoners with us, and therefore did then, and yet do, judge them not legal evidence against their fellow-prisoners. And I, being something hard of hearing and full of grief, none informing me how the Court took up my words, and therefore I had no opportunity to declare what I intended when I said they were of our company."

Touching words! "I being something hard of hearing and full of grief!" One queries whether the Court knew that she was a little deaf, and whether they urged the question of the foreman upon her so as to certainly know whether she had any reply to make. Of one thing we are sure. The judges urged upon the prisoners all questions implying their guilt with a vehemence and persistency that fully met the requirements of deaf ears. Here was a question on which the death penalty was suspended, and the questioner was permitted to return to the jurors without the prisoner being made to hear it, though she was only "something hard of hearing." That she was "full of grief" might have prompted a little pains in her behalf had her case not been prejudged by the Court, and all sympathy bestowed upon the diabolical accusers.

The jury came in with the solemn word "Guilty," and the sentence of death was not reluctantly pronounced by Lieutenant-Governor Stoughton, the Chief-Justice. Though the jurors did not hear her explanation, he and his associates did at a later moment, but it had no effect.

But the aggravating features of the case of Rebecca Nurse to herself and friends were not yet all developed. Governor Phipps interposed his executive clemency between her and the gallows. Forthwith the accusers "renewed their dismal outcries against her." Some Salem gentlemen came forward to represent to his Excellency the demands of those who believed her a witch.

Neal, in his history of New England, says there was in Salem, during the prevalence of the witchcraft *furor*, a Committee of Vigilance. They assumed the responsibility of hunting the witches, and advancing their prosecution. It is thought that this self-appointed committee of the public safety were the gentlemen who prevented the reprieve of Rebecca Nurse.

Thus, after imminent peril of life and alternations of hope and fear, this excellent woman—good wife and mother and true Christian—was executed on Witch Hill.

Scarcely less horrid than the hanging itself was the action of the Church to which she belonged, just after her conviction. It was, perhaps, but a sad consistency with their belief of her crime. The following is from the Church records:

"1692, *July* 3. After sacrament the elders propounded to the Church—and it was by a unanimous vote consented to—that our Sister Nurse, being a convicted witch by the Court, and condemned to die, should be excommunicated; which was accordingly done in the afternoon, she being present."

Her cup of wrong at the hands of her fellow-men was full.

CHAPTER XXII.

The Storm Raging.

THE Court reassembled on the 5th of August. They tried and condemned the following persons: George Burroughs, John Proctor and Elizabeth his wife, George Jacobs, Sen., John Willard, and Martha Carrier.

Our acquaintance with the Rev. Mr. Burroughs has become somewhat intimate. The wrongs he received in the settlement of his dues as the ex-Pastor of the Village Church; his sudden arrest and violent removal from the bosom of his family to the jail in Salem; his mock trial but genuine imprisonment, are all fresh in our memories. There is but little more of earthly sorrow that his persecutors can impose, since his home has been destroyed and his fair name blasted. The narrative of this *little more* is brief.

The following is a specimen of the spirit of his accusers and the Court which tried him, as well as the temper of the historian, Cotton Mather, who penned the lines: "It cost the Court a wonderful deal of trouble to hear the testimonies of the sufferers; for when they were going to give in their depositions they would for a long while be taken with fits, that made them quite incapable of saying any thing. The Chief Judge asked the prisoner who he thought hindered these witnesses from giving their testimonies, and he answered he supposed it was the devil. The honorable person then replied, 'How comes the devil so loath to have any testimony borne against you?' which cast him into very great confusion."

A modest, self-distrusting man, utterly confused by "the devil's legerdemain" enacted against him, had no sufficient answer in the judgment of the Court. "I know nothing of it; I am innocent," was an empty utterance to them. It was pursuing small game for their honors to cast upon their writhing victim, from their high place, a sneering perversion of the facts before them.

We have seen that at the preliminary trial the Court entertained against Burroughs questions concerning the baptism of his children, and his attendance at the Lord's Supper. They now inquired into his domestic relations. One Hannah Harris, a young woman who lived in his family at one time, testified that when she and Mrs. Burroughs had any discourse together in his absence, when he came home he scolded his wife, telling her that he knew what they said when he was abroad. She further testified to a scolding he gave his wife when her babe was but a week old, keeping her "at the door till she fell sick in the place and grew worse at night so that the said Hannah thought she would die."

Burroughs' wife's brother swore that he came home at one time and, finding him and his sister together, "fell to chiding his wife for talking to her brother about him, saying that he knew their thoughts, which the brother said was more than the devil knew; to which Burroughs replied that his God told him."

We may, in justice to the prisoner, remember that there was no one to cross-question these witnesses, and that, if they perverted Burroughs' words as much as the Chief-Justice did those spoken by Rebecca Nurse to her fellow-prisoners, we are ignorant of the just rendering of what he did say.

Witnesses were brought forward to prove that Burroughs had shown at sundry times supernatural strength. It was declared that he held out a gun, with seven feet barrel, "with only putting the forefinger of his right hand into the muzzle; that he had carried a barrel full of cider from a canoe to the shore." "An Indian present at the time did the same," answered the prisoner. The circle replied, "It was the Black Man, or the devil, who looks like an Indian." Some men swore that they passed Burroughs on one occasion, some considerable distance from home, they being on horseback and he afoot; and that they rode rapidly, but when they arrived he was there. He replied, "Another man accompanied me."

"It was the devil using the appearance of another man," shouted the girls.

Mr. Burroughs was, of course, brought in "guilty." He was hanged on Witch Hill.

John Proctor, too, we have previously seen. A neighbor to Giles Corey, he had at times allowed himself, we think, to judge the old man unjustly. But Proctor, as will be proved below, was a true man. His judgment was generally sound, and his contempt for the witchcraft acting of the girls had been expressed in his sharp manner. He had proposed to whip the devil out of Mary Warren, his servant girl.

The Rev. Mr. Wise of Ipswich, a man of learning and prominence, drew up an able paper in Proctor's behalf. Proctor had been brought up in his parish, and his family connections were there. The paper was signed by Mr. Wise and thirty-one others, all of Ipswich. It was addressed, in behalf of John Proctor and his wife, to "The honorable court of assistants now sitting in Boston." After more general remarks they declare: "What God may have left them to, we cannot go into God's pavilion clothed with clouds of darkness round about; but as to what we have ever seen or heard of them, upon our conscience we judge them innocent of the crime objected. His breeding hath been amongst us, and was of religious parents in our place, and by reason of relations and properties within our town, hath had constant intercourse with us. We speak upon our personal acquaintance and observation; and so leave our neighbors, and this our testimony on their behalf, to the wise thoughts of your honors."

Mr. Proctor's immediate neighbors of Salem Village signed a paper of similar import, testifying that, in their apprehension, "they lived Christ-like in their family."

In addition to these favorable words, it was shown in court that one of the witnesses had denied out of the court what she had sworn to before their honors, declaring that she must at the time have been "out of her head," and that she had never intended to accuse the prisoners at the bar.

Another of the girls acknowledged that she had sworn falsely; that what the girls said was "for sport;" "they must have some sport."

The sentence of death was passed upon John Proctor and his wife, Elizabeth Proctor. Two weeks before his execution on Witch Hill, while in prison at Salem, he wrote the letter addressed to "Mr. Mather, Mr. Allen, Mr. Moody, Mr. Willard, and Mr. Bailey." They were distinguished ministers of Boston. He writes in behalf of himself and fellow-prisoners, some of whom join him in signing the paper. He implores their assistance concerning "this our humble petition to his Excellency." He forcibly declares that nothing will satisfy the enmity of their accusers, and of the judges and jurors, but their innocent blood. He affirms that the magistrates, ministers, jurors, and all the people in general, are incensed against them "by the delusion of the devil." He makes a most telling point of the fact that the confessing witches who had testified against them had been most cruelly tortured into their confessions, and that his own son had been ineffectually abused to extort the same kind of lying. He truly adds, "These actions are very like the popish cruelties." He closes by begging that they may have a trial at Boston; and, if that cannot be granted, that the magistrates then on the bench be removed and others put in their place, and that some of the assistants be present at the trial.

This letter is respectful and well put. It has the pungent force of truth uttered without flattering circumlocution. But all availed nothing.

Two weeks after the execution of Proctor his condemned wife received to her bosom their new born child. An angel of mercy it was truly to the mother. Its coming postponed her execution, carrying the appointed day into a time when a voice had bidden the waves of passion be still, and she escaped the halter.

George Jacobs, Sen., bending with the weight of eighty-one years, supported by two crutches, next passes before us. We remember his unshrinking bearing and honest words on his former trial; his answer when told the girls charged him with being a witch, "Let them prove it, and I stand under it;" his appeal to the record of a thirty-three years' residence in Salem; and his solemn appeal to God in attestation of innocence. He had made his will before the witchcraft proceedings began. He was tried, condemned, and sentenced to die on the gallows. His only son, being accused of the same crime, had fled for his life to a foreign country. This son's insane wife was in prison under the same accusations, her little children being thrown upon the charity of the world; while her oldest daughter, Margaret, was an enforced confessor, bearing such testimony against all the family as was put into her mouth. We shall meet this Margaret again. In view of all this, as he lay in prison, one week before his death, the old man caused another will to be written. He gave his estates to his son George, and secured them to his male descendants. We shall be interested to visit his homestead, and make the acquaintance of the male descendant now owning and living in it.

Having thus calmly arranged his earthly business, we trust the wronged old man looked by faith in a crucified Redeemer for mercy from God, in whose presence he was soon to appear.

John Willard we shall recollect in connection with the strange sufferings of "old Bray Wilkins" on a certain election day, when the old man and his wife went to Boston and Dorchester, and met, at the latter place, the suspected Willard. The death of Wilkins' grandson will be remembered too—the boy who warned his father not to go to Boston with Willard, and who afterward died at the said Willard's hands, if the circle girls saw and testified truly. Willard was hanged for this. At his trial one of the possessed testified that she had seen him "suckle the apparition of two black pigs on his breast; and that he told them on the occasion that he had been a witch twenty years." Willard, having thus acted and testified before our veracious witnesses, "kneeled with other wizards, in prayer, to the black man, with a long crowned hat, and then vanished away."

Susanna Shelden first arrayed in ghastly procession the apparitions of murdered men, women, and children against Willard. But she brought into court a few "shining ones," most happily for the reader, who has seen so many "black men" and people "in winding sheets." "A shining man," most beautiful to behold, came and charged her with a message to the magistrates against Willard. This the witness declared that she could not do unless the shining one should "hunt Willard away," who was then choking her and threatening to cut her throat if she went. At this the shining one raises his hand, Willard vanishes, and the obedient messenger lives to deliver the message.

We cannot help suspecting that this "shining one" was the same old "black man" whom we have so often seen, as we know, on good authority, that he is sometimes "transformed into an angel of light." Susanna was undoubtedly imposed upon.

The four we have just noticed, namely, George Burroughs, John Proctor, George Jacobs, Sen., John Willard, with Martin Carrier, of whom we have no further information, were executed on the 19th of August.

On the 9th of September the Court met again and another installment was brought forward. Six persons at this time were tried and condemned. On the 17th following nine more received the same sentence. We shall detain the reader with a notice of only two of them, both old acquaintances, namely, Martha Corey and Mary Easty.

Mrs. Easty, it may be remembered, was a sister

of Rebecca Nurse, and Mrs. Corey, the wife of the notorious Giles Corey.

Mrs. Corey retained to the very last her self-reliance, her rejection of her deluded spiritual counsellors, and her trust in the Saviour whom she had consistently served.

The day after her sentence to death, the Church of the Village excommunicated her. Nathaniel Putnam, the two deacons, Ingersoll and Edward Putnam, were appointed a committee, in connection with their Pastor, to convey to her in Salem prison this decision of her brethren and sisters. They declare, or rather Mr. Parris, the Pastor, enters on the Church records, that they found her "very obstinate, justifying herself, and condemning all who had done any thing to her just discovery or condemnation. Whereupon, after a little discourse, (for her imperiousness would not suffer much,) and after prayer—which she was willing to decline—the dreadful sentence of excommunication was pronounced against her."

Calef says that "Martha Corey, protesting her innocency, concluded her life by an eminent prayer upon the ladder."

Mary Easty was imprisoned with her younger sister, Sarah Cloyse. While thus awaiting trial, these sisters addressed jointly a letter to the Special Court. They make the following points: First, as they were not allowed counsel, nor the privilege of speaking in their own defense, they beg the judges to direct them as they may have need—a reasonable but vain request. Secondly, as they, before God, declare their innocence of witchcraft or any scandalous act, they petition that those persons of good report who have long and well known them may be permitted to testify under oath concerning their lives. Thirdly, that the testimony of witches, or such as are supposed to be afflicted by witches, should not be used against them, "without other legal evidence concurring." Their closing words are solemnly significant: "We hope the honored Court and jury will be so tender of the lives of such as we are, who have lived for many years under the unblemished reputation of Christianity, as not to condemn them without a fair and equal hearing of what may be said for as well as against us."

For the judges to have granted their request under the third head, for a rejection of witchcraft testimonies when not accompanied by other legal evidence, would have been to acknowledge that all they had done was deeply criminal; and to have granted every thing else asked, when denying this, would have made the gift valueless. We do not know what the ministers did in response to this reasonable appeal, but we know that the Court a few days after brought Mrs. Easty to trial in the usual arbitrary, unjust way, and condemned her to death. Her sister, for some reason unknown, was never tried, and finally returned to her family.

Mrs. Easty, while awaiting the execution of her sentence, wrote to the Court and ministers a letter in behalf of her fellow-prisoners. She declares that she has learned to judge charitably of those awaiting trial by her own experience "of the wiles and subtilty of the accusers." She reminds them that she was cried out against, tried and imprisoned for a month, and then dismissed from custody, and that then the accusers renewed the outcries which had brought the fatal sentence. She nobly says, "The Lord above knew my innocency then, and likewise does now, as at the great day will be known to men and angels. I petition to your honors not for my own life, for I know I must die." She then plainly tells the judges that by her own innocence she knows that they are in the wrong way. She begs them to examine the afflicted persons strictly, and to keep them apart some time; and to try the confessing witches whom she knew had belied themselves. She adds, "I beg your honors not to deny this my humble petition from a poor, dying, innocent person."

God and not the Judges duly regarded these her dying words.

Nineteen persons had thus far suffered on Witch Hill—one in June, five in July, five in August, and eight in September. The prisons were yet full, the accusers as audacious and defiant as ever, and the Court unfaltering in its bloody course. But three days before the last executions a deed was done which was to rebound with destructive effect upon the heads of the accusers and judges. It was a deed of terrible persistency on the part of both oppressors and their victim.

CHAPTER XXIII.

Terrible Persistency.

GILES COREY has been frequently before the reader. He can now never be forgotten.

His situation while lying in jail awaiting a trial which he knew, if submitted to, would result in certain death, was very painful. He had, at first, added fuel to the witchcraft fire. His wife had, in some measure, suffered by the deposition he had allowed her enemies to extort from him. Crosby and Parker, two of his sons-in-law, following his bad example, had thrown their influence against her. And, most of all, his brief Christian life failed to give him that full measure of support which Rebecca Nurse and others derived from mature Christian graces. But great strength of purpose was yet remaining; whether prompted by a Christian faith, we leave the reader to judge.

He first drew up a conveyance of all his worldly estates and goods to his sons-in-law, William Cleeves and John Moulten, who had remained true to his wife and the right. This being duly signed, witnessed, and recorded, he settled down into his terrible resolution. He made up his mind not to plead when called into court, and thus to evade a trial. In this case his deed of conveyance would stand; otherwise, he was sure to be hanged, and his property to be taken by the State. He resolved to abide the consequences of refusing to plead, and such a death awaited him as few ever suffered.

Longfellow puts the following beautiful words into his mouth, which, we doubt not, are true to his spirit:

> "Now I have done with earth and all its cares;
> I give my worldly goods to my dear children;
> My body I bequeath to my tormentors,
> And my immortal soul to Him who made it.
> O God! who in thy wisdom doth afflict me
> With an affliction greater than most men
> Have ever yet endured or shall endure,
> Suffer me not in this last bitter hour
> For my pains of death to fall from thee!"

The poet introduces into the scene an old sailor by the name of Gardner, a friend of Corey's, who, just returned from sea, visits Corey's forsaken home. He describes a desolation that was but too real:

> "Here stands the house as I remember it,
> The four tall poplar trees before the door;
> The house, the barn, the orchard, and the well,
> With its moss-covered bucket and its trough;
> The garden with its hedge of currant bushes;
> The woods, the harvest fields; and, far beyond,
> The pleasant landscape stretching to the sea.
> But every thing is silent and deserted!
> No bleat of flocks, no bellowing of herds,
> No sound of flails, that should be beating now;
> Nor man, nor beast astir. What can this mean?
> [*Knocks at the door*—

What ho! Giles Corey! Hillo-ho! Giles Corey!
No answer but the echo from the barn,
And the ill-omened cawing of the crow,
That yonder wings his flight across the fields,
As if he scented carrion in the air.
* * * * * * *
"How often out at sea on stormy nights,
When the waves thundered round me, and the wind
Bellowed and beat the canvas, and my ship
Clove through the solid darkness like a wedge,
I've thought of him, upon his pleasant farm,
Living in quiet with his thrifty housewife,
And envied him, and wished his fate were mine!
And now I find him shipwrecked utterly,
Drifting upon this sea of sorceries,
And lost, perhaps beyond all aid of man."

Corey is supposed to have known what the old English law inflicted upon those who refused to answer when brought into court, and the question was put by the Judge, "Guilty or not guilty." It was to be laid upon his back, and a weight put upon his breast, increased at intervals while the question was repeated, until, if silence was persisted in, the life was crushed out. In the language of the law, "A strong and great pain" (*peine forte et dure*) was inflicted. While awaiting this dread issue Gardner visits him in prison:

COREY. I am glad to see you, aye, right glad to see you.
GARDNER. And I most sorely grieved to see you thus.
COREY. Of all the friends I had in happier days,
You are the first, aye, and the only one,
That comes to seek me out in my disgrace!
And you but come in time to say farewell.
They've dug my grave already in the field.
I thank you. There is something in your presence,

I know not what it is, that gives me strength.
Perhaps it is the bearing of a man
Familiar with all dangers of the deep,
Familiar with the cries of drowning men,
With fire, and wreck, and foundering ships at sea!

GARDNER. Ah, I have never known a wreck like yours!
Would I could save you!

COREY. Do not speak of that.
It is too late. I am resolved to die.

GARDNER. Why would you die who have so much to live for?
Your daughters, and—

COREY. You cannot say the word.
My daughters have gone from me. They are married;
They have their homes, their thoughts, apart from me;
I will not say their hearts—that were too cruel.
What would you have me do?

GARDNER. Confess and live.

COREY. That's what they said who came here yesterday
To lay a heavy weight upon my conscience,
By telling me that I was driven forth
As an unworthy member of their Church.

GARDNER. It is an awful death!

COREY. 'Tis but to drown,
And have the weight of all the seas upon you.

GARDNER. Say something; say enough to fend off death
Till this tornado of fanaticism
Blows itself out. Let me come in between you
And your severer self with my plain sense;
Do not be obstinate.

COREY. I will not plead.
If I deny, I am condemned already
In courts where ghosts appear as witnesses,
And swear men's lives away. If I confess,
Then I confess a lie to buy a life
Which is not life, but only death in life.
I will not bear false witness against any,
Nor even against myself whom I count last.

GARDNER, (*aside.*) Ah, what a noble character is this!

COREY. I pray you do not urge me to do that
You would not do yourself. I have already
The bitter taste of death upon my lips;
I feel the pressure of the heavy weight
That will crush out my life within this hour;
But if a word could save me, and that word
Were not the Truth; nay, if it did but swerve
A hair's-breadth from the Truth, I would not say it!
GARDNER, (*aside.*) How mean I feel beside a man like this!
COREY. As for my wife, my Martha and my Martyr,—
Whose virtues, like the stars, unseen by day,
Though numberless, do but await the dark
To manifest themselves unto all eyes,—
She was the first won me from my evil ways,
And taught me how to live by her example,
By her example teaches me to die,
And leads me onward to the better life!"

The place and precise circumstances attending the execution by slow crushing of Giles Corey are not known. Tradition has designated an open field near the jail in Salem as the place. As to the facts attending this shocking act in the tragedy, we know that Corey's lips were closed to the bitter end, and that the authorities, equally persistent, relented not.

The poet has charitably put into Cotton Mather's lips, as he looks upon the disfigured corpse, lying in the field with the weight still upon it, the following prophetic words:

"O sight most horrible! In a land like this,
Spangled with Churches evangelical,
Inwrapped in our salvations, must we seek
In moldering statute-books of English courts
Some old forgotten law to do such deeds?
Those who lie buried in the Potter's Field

Will rise again, as surely as ourselves
That sleep in honored graves with epitaphs;
And this poor man, whom we have made a victim,
Hereafter will be counted as a martyr."

The day after the death of Corey, one of the judges in Salem received a letter from Sergeant Thomas Putnam. It declared that the night before his daughter Ann was nearly pressed to death by a specter tormentor, but, "through the goodness of a gracious God, she had, at last, a little respite." During this respite one appeared to her "in a winding-sheet," declaring that Giles Corey had pressed him to death with his feet; and that for this acceptable deed the devil had promised Giles he should not be hanged—a promise that he had fulfilled in leading him not to plead.

What comfort the Court obtained from this piece of information we do not know. But the reader will be glad to be informed that it was the last vision of the tragedy.

CHAPTER XXIV.

The Confessions of the Accused.

THE Court, after the execution of Corey, hurried off to the gallows the eight persons of whom we have spoken, including Mary Easty and Martha Corey, and then adjourned. They were to re-assemble on the first Tuesday of November; but they never met again. His Excellency, Governor Phipps, put his foot down and the Court went under. There were to be no more ghosts in Court, playing bloody pranks at the expense of the lives of some of the best citizens of the province. We breathe freer. We can now calmly study the disposal of the contending forces, review the manner and spirit of the conflict, examine sadly the battle-field, and note the calmer feelings of those who have been conspicuous in the fight. We may then visit the localities made memorable in its history.

The reader can but have noticed that one main element of power on the part of the prosecutors was the confessions of the accused. They used them with terrible potency against the condemned. Next to the apparent tortures, and wonderful visions of the circle, they were the material which fed the witchcraft flames among the people. Brattle says, after other evidence against the accused began to be questioned, "The great cry of many of his neighbors was, 'What! will you not believe the confessors? Will you not believe men and women who confess they have signed the devil's book, that they were baptized by the devil, and that they were at the mock-sacraments once and again? What! will you not believe that this is witchcraft, and that such and such men are witches, although the confessors do own and assert it?"

If any of the readers of this history have the same queries to propose, the answer to them will be found in the following pages of this chapter.

Six of the confessors of Andover gave, over their signatures, the history and character of their confessions. They will serve as a key to most others. A paper accompanied it, signed by fifty of their fellow-citizens, in which they speak of "the sober, godly, exemplary conversation" of these retracting confessors.

The confessors state in general terms the circumstances of the visit of the two circle girls at Andover, their accusations, their confirming fits, and alterations by the looks and touch of the accused. They then say: "Whereupon we were all seized as prisoners, by a warrant from the justice of the peace, and forthwith carried to Salem; and by reason of that sudden surprisal, we knowing ourselves altogether innocent of that crime, we were all exceedingly astonished and amazed, and consternated, and affrighted, even out of our reason; and our nearest and dearest relations, seeing us in that dreadful condition, and knowing our great danger, apprehended there was no other way to save our lives, as the case was then circumstanced, but by our confessing ourselves to be such and such persons as the afflicted represented us to be. They out of tenderness and pity persuaded us to confess what we did confess. And, indeed, that confession that it is said that we made was no other than what was suggested to us by some gentlemen, they telling us that we were witches, and they knew it, which made us think it was so; and our understandings, our reason, our faculties almost gone, we were not capable of judging of our condition. The hard measures they used with us rendering us incapable of making our defense, we said any thing and every thing which they desired. The most of what we said was but consenting to what they said. Some time after, when we were better composed, they telling us what we had confessed, we did profess that we were ignorant of such things; and we hearing that Samuel Wardwell had confessed and renounced his confession, and was quickly after condemned and executed, some of us were told we were going after Wardwell."

Of two of these six persons giving the above statement, Mary Osgood and Mary Tyler, we have some further account.

Mary Osgood's confessions of her witch character had been very minute, containing dates, places, circumstances of a specific character, and the names of confederates. It was just such a confession as was claimed at the time, by the friends of the prosecution, as one bearing on its face the stamp of truthfulness. But we may go behind the curtain and hear these confessors cross-questioned. In October, after, it will be recollected, the termination of the Special Court, Increase Mather came to Salem and conversed in prison with the confessing witches. Here is what Mrs. Osgood had to say:

"Being asked why she prefixed a time and spoke of being baptized, etc., about twelve years ago, she replied and said that when she owned a thing they asked the time, to which she answered that she knew not the time. But, being told that she did know the time, and must tell the time, and the like, she considered that about twelve years before (when she had her last child) she had a fit of sickness and was melancholy, and so thought that that time would be as proper a time to mention as any, and accordingly did prefix the said time. Being asked about the cat in the shape of which she had confessed the devil had appeared to her, etc., she replied that, being told that the devil had appeared to her, etc., (she being a witch,) she at length did own the devil had appeared to her; and, being pressed to say in what creature's shape he appeared, she at length did say it was in the shape of a cat. Remembering that, some time before her being apprehended, as she went out of her door she saw a cat; not that she any whit suspected the said cat to be the devil, in the day of it, but because some creature she must mention, and this came into her mind at that time."

The statement of Mrs. Tyler in reference to her confession, made also to Dr. Increase Mather, contains facts equally remarkable. She says that, while under arrest and on her way from Andover to Salem jail, she was attended by her brother Bridges. As they rode together "he kept telling her all along the way that she must needs be a witch since the afflicted accused her, and at her touch were raised out of their fits." He therefore urged her to confess. She, however, steadfastly resisted his entreaties, saying she knew nothing of witchcraft, and finally begged him to desist from his teasing. "However, when she came to Salem she was carried to a room; her brother on one side, and Mr. John Emerson on the other, did tell her that she was certainly a witch, and that she saw the devil before her eyes at that time; and, accordingly, Emerson would attempt with his hand to beat him away from her eyes; and they so urged her to confess that she wished herself in any dungeon rather than be so treated. Mr. Emerson told her once and again, 'Well, I see you will not confess! Well, I will now leave you; and then you are undone, body and soul forever.'"

Her brother constantly joined Emerson in the appeals, adding, "Sister, confess; you will not lie in so doing." To which she touchingly replied, "Good brother, do not say so; for I shall lie if I confess, and then who shall answer unto God for my lie?" The brother argued that God would not suffer so many good men to be in error about this matter, adding the consideration, which was, no doubt, in his mind quite decisive, "You will be hanged if you do not confess."

This method of extorting a confession from her was continued by the well-intending brother and his friend until their victim breaks down, utterly exhausted in body and mind. She says, "I thought my life would go from me, and I became so terrified at length that I owned any thing propounded."

Having reached this point, the friends had only to put in the usual recitals about devil sacraments, trips through the air on sticks, tortures inflicted on the accusers, naming associates, times, and places, so that the whole would pass the profound scrutiny of their worships, and save Mrs. Tyler's neck from the halter.

Dr. Mather adds: "This she said, and a great deal more of a like nature; and all with such affection, sorrow, relenting, grief, and mourning, as that it exceeds any pen to describe and express the same."

The reader will recollect the case of George Jacobs, the infirm old man of eighty-one years, who had been hanged, with others, on the 19th of August. His son George had fled to escape the outcries of the circle girls. His granddaughter Margaret, under the pressure of her distracting circumstances, as she too was accused, had confessed, and turned against others, including her grandfather. She, however, retracted her confession in a most pathetic appeal to the Special Court.

After speaking of her arrest, and her terror at the fits of the girls and their recovery from them at her look and touch, and the positive declarations that were made to her that she was a witch, she adds: "They told me if I would not confess I should be put down into the dungeon and would be hanged; but if I would confess I should have my life. The which did so affright me, with my own vile, wicked heart, to save my life, made me make the like confession I did; which, may it please the honored Court, is altogether false and untrue. The very first night after I had made confession I was in such horror of conscience that I could not sleep for fear the devil should carry me away for telling such horrid lies. I was, may it please the honored Court, sworn to my confession, as I understand since; but then, at that time, was ignorant of it, not knowing what an oath did mean. The Lord, I hope, in whom I trust, out of the abundance of his mercy will forgive me my false forswearing of myself. What I said was altogether false against my grandfather and Mr. Burroughs, which I did to save my life and have my liberty. But the Lord, charging it to my conscience, made me in so much horror that I could not contain myself before I had denied my confession, which I did, though I saw nothing but death before me—choosing rather death with a quiet conscience than to live in such horror which I could not suffer. Upon my denying my confession I was committed to close prison, where I have enjoyed more felicity in spirit, a thousand times, than I did before my enlargement."

The day after the execution of her grandfather, Margaret wrote to her father, "from the dungeon in Salem prison," an affectionate letter. It is of the same import as the above. She relates the horror of feeling she had experienced after the confession "made through the magistrates' threatenings," and the peace of mind at her recantation, though she regarded her death on the gallows as certain and near. In her closing lines she says, "Dear father, let me beg your prayers to the Lord on my behalf, and send us a joyful and happy meeting in heaven."

It is pleasant to know that Margaret's temporary illness caused her trial to be postponed. While she waited its arrival, knowing that a trial meant condemnation and death, the Court itself was condemned, and she escaped.

The worthless character of the confessions appears in still another form. Sarah Churchill, the servant-girl of George Jacobs, who had played a bitter part as an accuser against her master and others, had moments of relentings. In these she shows the true source of her confessions of witchcraft. Just after, as it is believed, the old gentleman's commitment, the following deposition was made concerning her by Sarah Ingersoll: "Seeing Sarah Churchill after her examination, she came to me crying and wringing her hands, seeming to be much troubled in spirit. I asked her what she ailed? She answered she had undone herself. I asked her in what? She said in belying herself and others in saying she had set her hand to the devil's book, whereas, she said, she never did. I told her I believed she had set her hand to the book. She answered, crying, and said, 'No, no, no; I never, I never did!' I asked her then what made her say she did? She answered because they threatened her, and told her they would put her into the dungeon, and put her along with Mr. Burroughs. Thus several times she followed me up and down, telling me that she had undone herself in belying herself and others. I asked her why she did not deny she wrote it. She told me because she had stood out so long in it that now she durst not. She said also that if she told Mr. Noyes but once she had set her hand to the book he would believe her; but if she told the truth and said she had not set her hand to the book a hundred times he would not believe her."

The chapter on Confessions discloses the fact that, while very excellent persons of position and character failed to get a patient hearing in favor of the accused, the magistrates were willing to accept testimony from very humble confessors. They arrested a low woman by the name of Carrier, taking four of her children into confinement with her. When brought into court one of them, a child eight years of age, confessed being a witch, charging her mother with the crime of compelling her to sign the book. The Court carried her through the larger part of the witchcraft catechism, the questions of which she answered in the approved manner. Another child of Carrier was put upon the stand and by leading questions made to accuse herself, a brother, and her mother.

It is not strange that the wretched mother, evidently without Christian meekness, should have been provoked to resentment, when placed upon her own examination. The magistrate, as usual, assumed her guilt. She denied it. A circle girl said she then had the black man upon whom she looked. "What black man did you see?" asks the Judge. "I saw no black man but your own presence," was the sharp reply. But she trifled with her own life. Martha Carrier was hanged.

A poor, ignorant negro slave by the name of Candy was, in another case, put through the usual questions, to which she readily gave the desired answers. The following will serve as a specimen:

"Candy, are you a witch?"

"Candy no witch in her country. Candy's mother no witch. Candy no witch Barbadoes. This country mistress give Candy witch."

This intelligent witness was "improved" against her mistress.

The most painful fact connected with the confessing witches remains to be told. Some of them were tortured into confession. John Proctor, while lying in jail, wrote a letter to the leading ministers in Boston, begging their good offices with the Governor in his own and his fellow-sufferers' behalf. He said there were five persons in jail with him who had confessed themselves to be witches. He said two of the five were Carrier's sons, and that they were tied "neck and heels, till the blood was ready to come out of their noses;" and that on this account they confessed what they never did, accusing falsely also their mother.

Proctor further said that when his son William was being examined he refused to confess, and that consequently he was "tied neck and heels until the blood gushed out of his nose;" and that he was told he would be so tortured twenty-four hours if he did not confess. The young man, however, persisted, and, through the interference of one of his tormentors, he was relieved.

We are not told by whose authority these tortures were applied. In the absence of any explicit declaration we would believe them done by irresponsible parties. They fit well the historical character of the "Vigilance Committee" of which Neal speaks. Gentlemen composing these self-appointed custodians of the public safety are not wont to have bowels of compassion. We have seen a softer kind of torture offered by the teasings of mistaken friends, and the overbearing, protracted, and oft-repeated examinations of the judges.

Thomas Brattle, a rich merchant, whose name has been perpetuated by one of the streets in Boston, witnessed the doings of the Special Court. We have his account of the witchcraft proceedings in the fifth volume of the "Massachusetts Historical Society" publications. He says, speaking of the confessors: "Some of them denied their guilt and maintained their innocency for above eighteen hours, after most violent, distracting, and dragooning methods had been used with them to make them confess." He declares, further, that more than one of the confessors has said with many tears "that they thought their lives would have gone out of their bodies, and wished they might have been cast into the lowest dungeon rather than be tortured with such repeated buzzings, and chuckings, and unreasonable urgings as they were treated withal."

Brattle again refers to the subject, saying that "the confessors do very often contradict themselves;" "even the judges themselves have, at some times, taken these confessors in flat lies or contradictions even in the courts; by reason of which one would have thought that the judges would have frowned upon the said confessors, discarded them, and not minded one tittle of any thing they said; but, instead thereof, as sure as we are men, the judges vindicate the confessors and salve their contradictions by proclaiming that the devil takes away their memory and imposes upon their brain."

Brattle conclusively argues that if even in the judges' estimation the devil imposes upon the brains of these confessors no man of sense will regard their confessions.

It is a fact worthy of note that out of the fifty-five confessors none, except those who recanted their confessions, were hanged.

Of the confessors who did not recant, or of whose recantations no record is preserved, Brattle says: "They are possessed, I reckon, with the devil, and afflicted as the children are, and therefore not to be regarded as to any thing they say of themselves or others."

Having thus been behind the scenes with the confessors, observing their distracted state of mind under the bewildering circumstances in which they were placed, and witnessing the methods used which wearied out their bodily and physical strength, besides the tortures applied to the bodies of some, we shall have no difficulty in disposing of their testimony.

CHAPTER XXV.

The Collapse.

WE have seen that the Special Court, which dispensed terror and death during its short existence, dissolved suddenly; and that the fury of the witchcraft conflict subsided at the same time. There were deeply interesting causes for these results, into which we shall briefly look.

Governor Phipps alludes to his agency in the dismissal of the Court in a letter to the Home Government. He says: "I was, almost the whole time of the proceedings, abroad in the service of their majesties in the eastern part of the country, and depended upon the judgment of the Court as to a method of proceeding in cases of witchcraft; but when I came home I found many persons in a strange ferment of dissatisfaction, which was increased by some hot spirits which blew up the flame; but on inquiry into the matter I found the devil had taken upon him the name and shape of several persons who were doubtless innocent, and, to my certain knowledge, of good reputation."

The use, then, which had been made of the specter testimony had stirred up "a strange ferment." A sharp controversy had been going on in the province on this matter from the beginning of the prosecutions, which had increased in boldness on the part of specter opposers, so that, when the Governor returned, about the middle of October, 1692, from his war with the Indians on the coast of Maine, there was a buzzing about his ears. He was greatly moved by what he heard. When fears were expressed by old friends concerning the fall of the Special Court, he repeated with emphasis, "Let it fall." He went further. He adds, in his letter to the Home Minister: "I have also put a stop to the printing of any discourses one way or the other that may increase the needless disputes of people upon this occasion, because I saw a likelihood of kindling an inextinguishable flame if I should admit any public or open contests."

The Legislature convened October 26. It had in it a reactionary element. Some of its members had personally suffered by the pestilential breath of the circle girls; more had been wounded through condemned or accused friends. Dudley Bradstreet, son of Governor Bradstreet, was a member from Andover. He and his wife had been obliged to fly to save their lives. A member from Haverhill was connected with a family three of whose members had been brought to the bar of the Court. A member from Salisbury was son-in-law of Mary Bradbury, on whom the death sentence had been passed. These and many others were at the seat of government with a defiant spirit of opposition.

Brattle speaks of the wide-spread opposition which was showing itself. Writing in October, he says: "This you may take for a truth, that there are several about the Bay, men for understanding, judgment, and piety inferior to few if any in New England, that do utterly condemn the said proceedings, and do freely deliver their judgment in the case to be this, namely, that these methods will utterly ruin and undo poor New England. I shall nominate some to you, namely, the Hon. Simon Bradstreet, Esq., our late Governor, the Hon. Thomas Danforth, late Deputy Governor, the Rev. Mr. Increase Mather, and the Rev. Samuel Willard."

He further says that, excepting Mr. Hale, Mr. Noyes and Mr. Parris, "the reverend elders almost throughout the whole country are very much dissatisfied." One judge, he says, had left the Court "dissatisfied," being unwilling to have any official connection with it. Many, both of the retired and active justices in the Province, were showing their hands in opposition. Some of those holding positions as magistrates in Boston were threatening to resign rather than to be used as tools of the accusing girls.

We take great satisfaction in this uprising of such numbers of the people, judges, clergy, and men of position in the State, to arrest at this point the destroying angel of witchcraft. Had it developed during the earlier legal investigation so as to have prevented the existence of the death-dealing Special Court, our satisfaction would have been deeper.

There was a reason for dissatisfaction on the part of some, at the proceedings in Salem, worthy of special note. We must charitably believe it was only one among many reasons of a more disinterested nature. The accusers, prompted no doubt in part by their great success, had attained to a profound contempt for excellence of character and prominence of position in those at whom they chose to aim their poisoned arrows. The wife of Governor Phipps had been struck by one. The Rev. Samuel Willard of Boston was selected as a victim—the arrow being placed in the string and brought to the sight; but it was struck from the bow by one of the judges, who told the accusing girl she had mistaken the person. A mother-in-law of one of the acting magistrates; a member of the family of the President of Harvard College; the wife of the Rev. Mr. Hale of Beverly; a venerable minister in Andover; all felt the far-reaching power of their shafts. They were becoming as relentless as the destroying angel sent by God against Egypt, and they promised that there should not be a home nor a family in which there should not be an exceeding bitter cry for one slain —even from the Governor's mansion to the lowest cabin of the poor. It was esteemed no doubt by the judges a solemn duty to sit in judgment on the value of the accusers' testimony, and to give it weight against the prisoners; but to be the victims of their accusations was another thing. Mr. Hale did not maliciously, but only blindly act when he aided by his great influence to give wings to their words; but when they flew into the sacred enclosure of his own home and struck his wife, who had been eminent for her purity of heart and usefulness of life, the scales fell from his eyes.

There were parties every-where, it may be presumed, like the Jews in Queen Esther's day, who were ready, when the arm of persecution faltered, to assail their assailants. The Andover people were especially plucky at this crisis. They obtained warrants and proceeded to arrest the accusers for slander. These "pests" soon found that there was more "sport" in smiting than in being smitten. They at once ceased to accuse. They cried for quarter and withdrew from the contest. But they had no reason to complain, though their occupation was gone. Their "amazing fits" ceased. All torturing and affrighting ghosts vanished into thin air. "When the spectral testimony was discredited the afflictions of the afflicted ceased" is a declaration that comes to us in substance from both their friends and their enemies.

Bently says: "Witchcraft soon proved itself to be an error to be corrected in the public opinion and not in courts of justice. . . . As soon as the judges ceased to condemn, the people ceased to accuse. Just as after a storm, the people were astonished to see the light break out on them again. Terror at the violence and guilt of the proceedings succeeded instantly to the conviction of blind zeal, and what every one had encouraged all professed to abhor. Few dared to blame other men, because few were innocent. They who were most active remembered that they had applauded. The guilt and the shame became the portion of the country, while Salem had the infamy of being the place of the transaction."

We may now walk over the battle-field and mark the track along which the conflict raged. Twenty had been slain; two besides had died in prison. The good name of many excellent people had been for the time blasted. A husband and wife had accused each other; parents had acknowledged their children bewitched, and children had sworn away, in distraction and terror, the lives of their parents. Of course many homes, where before peace and joy had dwelt, were filled with discord and wretchedness. Confidence, the bond of union, had been broken, and distrust had taken its place. The enemy whom bolts and solid walls could not keep from the dwelling was feared more than the open, defiant foe; and with reason, for the former smote in the dark. To the children especially the day as well as the night was made hideous by frightful sights and sounds with which their distempered imaginations filled every place.

A less but no small evil was the loss, to a great extent, of the means of a comfortable subsistence. A spring, summer, and fall had been struck from the year. The hand of industry had been paralyzed. No harvest had been gathered, because no seed had been planted. Trade had stagnated or was turned from its customary channels, and business in general received a shock from which it was slow in recovering. Taxes, which before were esteemed heavy, were greatly increased. The accused were plundered by the government to pay in part the extraordinary expense attending their examinations. A few facts will show how this was done. John Proctor, writing to some of the ministers of Boston from his prison, says, "They have already undone us in our estates."

The old man George Jacobs had received the death sentence, but this was not enough: "The sheriff and officers came and seized all he had; his wife had her wedding-ring taken from her, but, with great difficulty, obtained it again. She was forced to buy provisions of the sheriff, such as he had taken, toward her support, which, not being sufficient, the neighbors in charity relieved her."

His son, George Jacobs, Jun., who fled to save his life, whose wife and daughter were imprisoned at a cost to him "of twelve pounds in money to the officers, besides other charges," and whose property was utterly destroyed, at a later period returned an inventory of what the sheriff took from the parental homestead. It runs thus: "Five cows, fair large cattle; eight loads of English hay taken out of the barn; twelve barrels of cider; sixty bushels of Indian corn; a mare; five swine; two feather-beds, furniture, rugs, blankets, sheets, bolsters and pillows; two brass kettles; twelve shillings in money; a large gold thumb ring; a quantity of pewter; besides an abundance of small things—meat in the house, fowls, chairs, etc.—took clear away."

Many such bills were afterward presented to the government.

But there is a more painful feature of this legalized plundering. Persons arrested were compelled to pay all charges of every kind. Their board, fuel, clothes, traveling expenses to their place of imprisonment and from jail to jail when removed, all came in to swell the ruinous expense levied upon their estates or friends. Nor was this all. Fees were required at every turn—a fee to the clerk of the court, a fee for a reprieve, a fee for a discharge, and even a fee to the hangman! One man paid two pounds and ten shillings to get the body of his mother who died in prison.

Added to these demands of the law was the loss in some cases to the prosecuted from the unrestrained freedom of the mob. "As soon as Phillip English was apprehended, his house was opened and every thing movable became free plunder to the multitude."

It is not strange that the accounts speak of "a diminished population," and of "shadows cast over a broad surface, darkening the condition of generations."

Notwithstanding the witchcraft conflict had been so disastrous to the whole community, and its defeat in the fall of the Special Court so marked, the prosecuting party showed for awhile faint efforts of life.

The regular court, called the Superior Court, was held in Salem in January, 1693. Lieutenant-Governor Stoughton was Chief-Justice. Specter evidence was forbidden. Calef says, "At these trials some of the jury made inquiry of the Court what account they ought to make of the specter evidence, and received for answer—'*As much as of chips in wort!*'"

Though the ghosts were ordered out of the court, the Grand Jury indicted fifty persons for witchcraft, twenty of whom were tried, and three condemned. It is thought the Court made free use of the confessors in finding even these guilty. In the subsequent sessions, which continued until May, the trials uniformly resulted in acquittals; at this time the plucky Governor came down upon the proceedings again, and by proclamation opened all the prison doors to the alleged witches, setting free not only the suspected but even those under the sentence of death. It was a wonderful jail-delivery! One hundred and fifty were set at liberty at this time—at least such of them as could pay their jail bills. How many were arrested in all is not certainly known; it must have been several hundred.

But we may not fully understand the effects of this wild witchcraft ferment unless we scrutinize them somewhat in detail. This we shall attempt to do in the next chapter.

CHAPTER XXVI.

Incidents of the Trials and Executions.

WE have spoken of the desolated track of the delusion. We have noticed its annoying, often ruinous effects upon those committed to prison, though not condemned. As in a wreck by a storm at sea, or a collision of railroad cars, there are not only the aggregate and individual losses which belong to the history of such events, but interesting personal incidents; so in the witchcraft storm and consequent catastrophe. We shall present a few of them in illustration of our story.

Some of those committed to prison who had influential friends, or that special friend, wealth, were allowed, under bonds, a private custody. William Hobbs, whose trial we have noticed, was bailed out by two of his neighbors. When the day of his trial arrived they did not think his appearance at the Court safe, so they generously paid the bond—two hundred pounds. This undoubtedly saved his life. At the session of the Superior Court in May of the next year, the specters having disappeared, Hobbs appeared, was discharged, and the money of his friends returned by the officials.

The reader will recollect the case of Captain

John Alden of the provincial navy, whose personal account of the rough handling he received by the circle we have given. He escaped from the Boston jail in the middle of September, when condemnations were being made in large installments, and the danger was imminent. He fled to Duxbury and was secreted by his friends. He made his appearance among them late at night. They were alarmed at his sudden and untimely presence, and asked an explanation. He replied, "I am flying from the devil and the devil is after me." He too reported in person to the Court when it had recovered its senses, and was discharged.

If there was energy manifested in this and many other cases in flying from the accusers, there was, as we have seen, a hot haste often on the part of the prosecuting party. This is further illustrated by the following statements in reference to the arrest of Mary Easty. It will be recollected that she had been arrested and committed to prison. For some reason she was soon after set at liberty. As soon as she was again in the bosom of her now happy family, and while their tears of joy still moistened their faces, the girls opened upon her their most destructive enginery, intensified in power by their wrath at her escape.

On the 20th of May Mercy Lewis, being at the house of John Putnam, had fits, and experienced tortures not exceeded, if we may credit the accounts, in the agony suffered or the peril of life experienced, by any which were endured in the whole of that eventful period of Satan's unchaining. Her tormentor flaunted a winding-sheet in her face, brought chains and coiled them about her tender neck with witch brutality; choked and crushed her until life faintly and feebly lingered in its earthly casket. Ann Putnam was sent for to see who hurt Mercy. Ann came, accompanied by Abigail Williams. This was in the forenoon of May 20th. The messenger had traveled a mile and a quarter. He was started again for Mary Walcot, another ride of three miles. Miss Walcot hurried along, of course, and had scarcely given her opinion when away the messenger flew for Elizabeth Hubbard, another three miles. Evening came on, and with it neighbors and friends from far and near hurried to the spot, gathered by rumors of the more than death agonies of Mercy Lewis. The girls with one voice shrieked, *Mary Easty!* They clearly saw her and her accomplices torturing Mercy. So plainly did they describe each Satanic act of the witches, and so vividly did they portray the form and spirit of their coming with "book," "winding-sheet," and "chain," that the pitying spectators seemed to hear and see. It was eight o'clock. Messengers go to the Town for a warrant against Mary Easty, and return. Another eight miles has been traveled. Armed with this fatal authority, Marshal Herrick, a young man of knightly bearing and fiery zeal, spurs on his panting horse until he reins up at Isaac Easty's in Topsfield. His wife, Mary, is torn from her bed and distracted family, and Herrick, at midnight, is again at the bedside of poor, suffering, and, as he fears, dying Mercy Lewis. Another six miles has been accomplished. While the darkness so fitting to the transaction still rests upon the forest through which she has ridden, Mrs. Easty is lying, chained, in a dungeon of Salem jail. At midnight sleeping in unsuspecting security under her own roof, surrounded with her family; now at least seven miles away, and treated as the worst of criminals. Her husband, referring to the transaction twenty years afterward forcibly exclaimed, "It was a hellish molestation."

The husband of Elizabeth How was blind. They had two daughters, Mary and Abigail. When the wife and mother was under arrest, one of them accompanied their father twice a week to visit their mother, and to bear to her within her gloomy cell the assurances of their abiding love. Their house was off the public road; the distance considerable, and the exposure to annoyances by the way from excited and bewildered travelers very great. But their affection knew no obstacles. They exhausted their humble means in relieving her necessities. When she was condemned to die, one of them traveled to Boston and begged in vain for her life. As we have seen, she was hanged, but her last moments were blessed by these tokens of love, and by their declaration that their "honored mother was as innocent of the crime charged as any person in the world."

There is a touching story of the heroism of a young man in behalf of his mother. He succeeded in securing her escape from jail, and secreted her in the woods. Not daring to trust her sacred person in any known habitation during the raging of the witchcraft storm, he built for her a wigwam in the depth of the forest. One of her limbs was injured in her efforts to clear the prison wall, yet here he fed, nursed, and watched her until the danger had passed away.

In noticing the incidents of the conflict, we should do great injustice to the subject if we did not present those concerning the sufferers in prison and the victims on the gallows. Manly and Christian fortitude have seldom in the history of the world been put to a severer test than by the treatment these persons received. The sudden surprisal of some of them by the officers of the law, in the midst of their quiet and happy homes; the strange nature of the charge against them; the arbitrary methods and cruel spirit of the Court; the plundering of their goods, and the imposing upon them the expenses of their arrest and imprisonment; the crowded, poorly furnished, and scantily provisioned condition of the jails; the virtuous and depraved made companions in suffering—all these facts made an accumulated weight upon body and mind which no common fortitude could sustain.

There was to *some*, perhaps, one consideration more crushing than all besides. It was this: Their consciousness of innocence and their personal views of the evidence of their guilt were in conflict. They would, as readily as any of the Court, have condemned others on the proof of guilt brought against themselves. They believed in all that the Court believed, and only had what the Court could not have, a consciousness of innocence. The Rev. Mr. Burroughs, whose case in many respects was harder than that of any other, seems to have been in just this perplexity. The exhibitions against him were to his mind "an amazing providence." He knew nothing of it. He declared that he did not blame the judges. He was cut off from every outward support. He turned for strength and comfort in the dark hour to God "who only giveth songs in the night."

The destitute, suffering condition of those imprisoned is referred to in an address of seven citizens of Andover to the General Court, concerning their wives and children, praying that they might be released on bonds, "to remain as prisoners in their own houses, where they may be more tenderly cared for." They speak of them as, "A company of poor distressed creatures, as full of inward grief and trouble as they are able to bear up in life withal." They refer to their want of proper food and sufficient shelter from the cold, "which may dispatch such out of the way that have not been used to such hardships." They also speak feelingly of the ruinous demands made for the support of these prisoners upon their families.

But we need not pursue this painful part of our history further. This much is due to these sufferers, that the Christian patience with which the most of them endured their wrongs, and the joy they experienced at the proclamation which opened their prison doors, may be appreciated by the reader.

The incidents connected with those who suffered the death penalty demand attention, and will be found of peculiar interest. Brattle, who was present in Salem during the trial and execution of at least some of them, thus speaks of their last moments: "As to the late executions, I shall only tell you that, in the opinion of many unprejudiced, considerate, and considerable spectators, some of the condemned went out of the world not only with as great protestations, but also with as good shows of innocency, as men could do.

"They protested their innocency as in the presence of the great God, whom forthwith they were to appear before; they wished, and declared their wish, that their blood might be the last innocent blood shed upon that account. With great affection they entreated C. M. (Cotton Mather) to pray with them. They prayed that God would discover what witchcrafts were among us; they forgave their accusers; they spake without reflection upon jury and judges for bringing them in guilty and condemning them; they prayed earnestly for pardon for all *other* sins and for an interest in the precious blood of our dear Redeemer, and seemed to be very sincere and upright, and sensible of their circumstances on all accounts; especially Proctor and Willard, whose management of themselves from the jail to the gallows, and whilst at the gallows, was very affecting and melting to the hearts of some considerable spectators whom I could mention."

The words and spirit of Burroughs in his last

moments were eminently Christ-like. He made a speech upon the ladder of the gallows in which he declared his innocence. The solemnity and seriousness of his expressions excited the admiration of all present. His prayer was uttered with such well-chosen words, composure, and fervency of spirit, that the spectators were melted to tears, and some of them seemed ready to hinder his execution. Most fittingly his last words were those of the Lord's Prayer.

The accusing girls, following their victim to the very last moment of his mortal life, were moved to jealousy by this evidence of his innocence. They tried to break its force by saying that the Black Man stood and dictated to him.

The parting interview of Sarah Easty with her husband, children, and friends, was characterized by Christian dignity and affection. Her words and sweetness of spirit drew tears from all who were present.

The persons executed were carried in a cart from the jail to Witch Hill. The eight executed in September made one load. The distance was considerable, as we shall see when we visit the localities, and, no doubt, the roads rough and the ascent of the hill difficult. It is not surprising that the cart was for some time "set," aggravating the painfulness of their situation.

The bodies of the executed seem to have been buried by the Sheriff on or near the place of execution. Sheriff Corwin, in his official return in the case of Bridget Bishop, which has been preserved, after stating the fact of having hanged her, adds, "and buried her on the spot," but drew his pen across the words, as if the statement were not necessary to the return. Declarations were made in print a few years after, of the bad treatment the bodies received at the hands of those charged with carrying into effect the sentence of the law; and tradition preserves the stories of the stealthy recovery of some of the bodies by their friends. We know that there was a fearful kind of insanity possessing at the time the minds of the people, including those in authority, concerning what was due a witch, whether living or dead. It was this that developed so many strange and painful incidents, with which our story is illustrated.

CHAPTER XXVII.

An Important Inquiry.

WE have endeavored to describe the ruin produced by the witchcraft *furor*, illustrating it by incidents of personal experiences. Faint indeed has been our portrayal of what can never be fully apprehended. But the sad scenes and bitter griefs which have come to our notice naturally prompt the inquiry, Who were responsible? We may not in truth write, as reporters often do of collisions on the public thoroughfares by cars and by steamers, "Nobody was to blame." We lose the benefits of the moral lesson of great public calamities unless we candidly and carefully note individual responsibility for their occurrence.

Yet the inquiry in this case is both delicate and difficult. We will not affect to hold a plummet equal to its mysterious depth. But we may present some facts which will aid the reader to a judgment concerning the moral relations of the principal actors, to the final consequences.

The ministers of the province, especially those of Salem, Boston, and their vicinities, appear prominently among these actors. It is not easy to give their true position, but we shall endeavor to do it with painstaking and candor.

We have presented, in connection with the account of the Special Court, the substance of a letter to the authorities signed by twelve prominent ministers, in which their judgment is stated of the method which ought to be adopted in the legal proceedings. We refer the reader to that account.* They advised that "very critical and exquisite caution" be used in the admission of spectral evidence. Cotton Mather, who wrote the letter above noticed, and who claims to have held opinions on this point in common with his clerical brethren, says, in a letter to one of the judges, written in March, 1692, about the commencement of the examinations, "I must humbly beg you, in the management of the affair in your most worthy hands, you do not lay more stress upon pure specter testimony than it will bear." He further says that if there be "good legal evidence" that the specters of accused persons torment the afflicted, it may be used as presumptive, but not convicting proof of guilt. He declares it certain that devils have sometimes assumed the shape not only of innocent, but very virtuous persons.

Dr. Increase Mather, then President of Harvard College, wrote and published about the time of the witchcraft trials, "Cases of conscience concerning evil spirits personating men, etc." It bore the indorsement of fourteen ministers of Boston and vicinity. Of the afflicted persons he says: "What they affirm concerning others is not to be taken for evidence. Whence had they this supernatural

* Page 203.

sight? It must be either from heaven or from hell. If from heaven, let their testimony be received. But if they had this knowledge from hell, though there may possibly be truth in what they affirm, they are not legal witnesses; for the law of God allows of no revelation from any other spirit but himself, Isaiah viii, 19. It is a sin against God to make use of the devil's help to know that which cannot be otherwise known; and I testify against it as a great transgression which may justly provoke the Holy One of Israel to let loose devils on the whole land, Luke iv, 38."

He says again: "The first case that I am desired to express my judgment in is this, Whether it is not possible for the devil to impose on the imaginations of persons bewitched, and cause them to believe that an innocent, yea, that a pious person does torment them, when the devil himself does it; or whether Satan may not appear in the shape of an innocent and pious, as well as of a hurtful and wicked person, to afflict such as suffer by diabolical molestations. The answer to the question must be affirmative."

A person of some prominence in Boston, having a sick child, carried it to Salem to the circle girls, to see what they would say of its disease. They, of course, saw specters of certain persons whom they named, afflicting it. The father returned home and attempted to get warrants to arrest the persons represented. President Mather interfered and reproved him sharply. "What!" said he, "is there not a God in Boston, that you should go to the devil in Salem for advice?"

We have given, in our chapter on "Strange Things," the history of Elizabeth Knapp of Groton, whose case the Rev. Mr. Willard managed and cured without the aid of courts.

In 1692 he published a tract with this title: "Some Miscellaneous Observations on our present Debates respecting Witchcraft."* In it we have Mr. Willard's opinions concerning the right method of trying witches, as opposed to that of the Judges. He argues that for conviction there must be, first, a fact done and proved; second, indubitable evidence that the fact proves the crime charged; third, a clear legal proof that the accused did the fact. By "legal proof" he means, first, a confession of one not frightened nor forced into it, and in his "right mind;" second, the testimony of two human witnesses to the same fact. By a human witness he means one who obtains his knowledge by "the natural use of his senses."

He argues that the afflicted are not competent witnesses because "they are possessed;" because they cannot give a full and clear testimony to the face of the prisoner "as required by law and reason;" because the alleged smiting down of the accusers by the accused, by their looks and motions, is more than can be proved; because the judges themselves allow that the devils sometimes

* This tract has been very scarce, and known only to antiquaries. It was published entire in the July number of the "Congregational Quarterly," 1869.

take away the memory of the afflicted, so disqualifying them to speak; and, finally, because their testimony is not human, and so not legal. He pointedly declares that the judges must believe that all that are accused are witches, or that the afflicted either lie or are deluded.

The ministers generally believed that "prayer is the powerful and effectual remedy against the malicious practices of devils and those that covenant with them." We have seen that at the commencement of the witchcrafts of Salem Village the ministers of the vicinity met at Mr. Parris' house for fasting and prayer in behalf of the afflicted. Cotton Mather declared that "prayer and faith was the thing which drew the devil from the Goodwin children;" and he recommends it in his letter to Judge Richards. Referring in his "Magnolia" to the witchcraft uprising at Salem, he says: "In fine, the country was in a dreadful ferment, and wise men foresaw a long train of dismal and bloody consequences. Hereupon they first advised that the afflicted might be kept asunder in the closest privacy; and one particular person, (whom I have cause to know,) in pursuance of this advice, offered himself, singly, to provide accommodations for any six of them, that so the success of more than ordinary power of prayer and fasting might, with patience, be experienced, before any other courses were taken."

We learn elsewhere that he, Cotton Mather, was that "one particular person," and we suppose he refers to the ministers as the "wise men" who "foresaw the dismal and bloody consequences."

We have dwelt thus in detail upon the "specter testimony," because the whole question of responsibility turned upon its use. With it and by it the witchcraft angel of death spread his wings on the blast. When it became of no more value than "chips in wort" the death angel disappeared.

We shall now show how the above-stated opinions of the clergy on this vital point were qualified by other statements, and by their application of it—or, at least, the application of it by some of them—to the occurring trials.

The reader will have noticed that the ministers uniformly insisted upon "critical and exquisite caution" in handling specter testimony, and never demanded a prohibition of its use. Mr. Willard came near making this demand; he utterly disallowed it except as an inquiry in cases of persons of previous bad life. Dr. Increase Mather, in immediate connection with his declaration that to *convict* a witch on spectral evidence is a "great transgression," says: "The devil's accusations may be so far regarded as to cause an inquiry into the truth of things." His son, Cotton Mather, when referring to the "odd effects" produced by the looks and touch of the accused upon the accusers, speaks of them as "things wherein the devils may as much impose upon some harmless people as by the representation of their shapes;" yet, in describing these "odd effects" as occurring in the trials, he speaks of them in graphic language as matters of fact. The following is an illustration: "When many of the accused came upon their examination, it was found that the demons, who had more than a thousand ways abusing of the poor afflicted people, had with a marvelous exactness represented them; yea, it was found that many of the accused but casting their eyes upon the afflicted, the afflicted, though their faces were never so much another way, would fall down and lie in a sort of swoon, wherein they would continue, whatever hands were laid upon them, until the hands of the accused came to touch them, and then they would revive immediately; and it was found that various kinds of natural actions done by many of the accused in or to their own bodies, as leaning, bending, or turning awry, or squeezing their hands, or the like, were presently attended by the like things preternaturally done upon the bodies of the afflicted, though they were so far asunder that the afflicted could not at all observe the accused."

He adds at the close of this account: "Flashy people may burlesque these things, but when hundreds of the most sober people in a country where they have as much mother wit certainly as the rest of mankind know them to be *true*, nothing but the absurd and forward spirit of Sadduceeism can question them. I have not yet mentioned so much as one thing that will not be justified, if it be required, by the oaths of more considerate persons than any that can ridicule these odd phenomena."

The point is that, while Mr. Mather believed

that the devil *could* deceive by these odd effects, those exhibited at the examinations are assumed to have been results of what was done by the accused upon the accusers, the very point denied by Mr. Willard but claimed by the judges. He thus establishes them as "presumptions," and they become practically decisive evidence of guilt. He affirms that the same use might be made of spectral representations, for "many witchcrafts had been fairly detected on inquiries provoked and begun by spectral exhibitions."

Again, in a letter written about the middle of June, 1692, at a most critical time of the proceedings, Cotton Mather, after emphasizing the fact that the devil might appear in any person's shape, even his own, says: "Nevertheless, a very great use is to be made of the spectral impressions upon the sufferers. They justly introduce and determine an inquiry into the circumstances of the person accused, and they strengthen other presumptions. When so much use is made of those things, I believe the use for which God intends them is made."

We learn, from Cotton Mather's letter to Judge Richards, referred to in another place, that among these "other presumptions," in his judgment, which gave weight to specter evidence, were wounds given to specters and received by witches; the discovery of "witch-marks" or teats on the bodies of the accused; and the water ordeal, for he says, "some might be found buoyant if the water ordeal were made upon them."

We have not been able to find any evidence that the magistrates of Salem followed this suggestion, by throwing the accused, with their thumbs and toes tied together, into the water, to see if they would float, after the manner of the "Witch-finder General." As to the presumption from witch-marks, Hutchinson says: "Some said the credulity was such that a flea-bite would pass well enough for a teat or devil's mark."

The way in which some of the ministers qualified and explained their views of spectral evidence is seen further by a statement made by Increase Mather in his "Cases of Conscience." He says: "I know that at a meeting of the ministers at Cambridge, August 1, 1692, there were seven Elders present besides the President of the College. The question then discoursed on was whether the devil may not sometimes have a permission to represent an innocent person as tormenting such as are under diabolical molestation? The answer, which they all concurred in, was in these words, namely, 'That the devil may sometimes have a permission to represent an innocent person as tormenting such as are under diabolical molestations, but that such things are rare and extraordinary, especially when such matters come before civil judicatures;' and that some of the most eminent ministers of the land who were not at that meeting are of the same judgment I am assured."

Cotton Mather in his "Wonders of the Invisible World" refers to this meeting, and says it uttered the sense of other ministers "eminently cautious and judicious." These explanations of their position on spectral evidence account for the language of the ministers in the second article of their advice to the authorities. They there "with all thankfulness acknowledge the success which a merciful God" had given to the endeavors of the magistrates "to detect abominable witchcrafts." The readers know what the methods were which the magistrates used to secure this "success."

CHAPTER XXVIII.

Court Scenes and the Judges.

THE acting magistrates have been before us in their official conduct. They have not made the most favorable impression by the manner in which they have discharged their duties in the court-room. Their bearing toward the trembling prisoners has been harsh and oppressive. There has been scarcely a concealment of the fact that condemnation preceded trial. No counsel was allowed the prisoners, and friends expressed their sympathy for them in the presence of authority at the peril of their lives. The examinations in many cases were hasty, and the execution followed swift upon condemnation. The crowd of amazed spectators in the court-room listened with profound interest. The Judges, with solemn dignity occupying an elevated seat, attended by other office-bearers, with the afflicted girls close at hand, flanked by John Indian, awaited the prisoner. Her approach sent the girls into convulsive fits, and John Indian into ground tumblings. The piercing, agonizing cries of the girls filled the court-room, and reached the ears of the excited people without. Their eyes set in their heads, their distorted countenances as they writhed in pain, filled the Court and spectators with awe and grief. The prisoner was blindfolded and made to touch the sufferers, and immediately they were well; or, if they did not instantly recover, as was usually the case, the Judge pronounced them well. Now came the battle between the accused and accusers, or the contest in which it was assumed by the Court that the prisoner knocked down the witnesses by a glance of her eye, a pressure of her hand, though several feet off—by the movement of a foot, or the twisting of the body. The patient Court lost hours of precious time by this annoying wickedness of the arraigned. It was to them the consummation of criminality to "act witchcraft in the presence of authority." They ordered the prisoner to be bound in the presence of the Court and people. An officer was placed at either side of her to prevent Satanic acting. She was commanded to look away from the accused, while, at the intervals of composure on the part of the witnesses, the Judge demanded of the prisoner to explain these wonderful phenomena. "Who hurts these?" "Can you tell what afflicts them?" which meant, Clear yourself from responsibility for this witchcraft—Prove your innocence! Generally the trembling prisoner was wholly at loss, and as surprised and awed by these sights and sounds as was the Court and gaping crowd, and could only say, meekly, "It is an amazing and humbling providence; I know nothing of it," acquiescing in the justice of a sentence of guilty although conscious of innocence. Occasionally a prisoner, provoked and stung by the injustice of the magistrate and the impertinence of an under officer or bystander, answered, "How should I know? don't ask me!" or, being keenly wounded, retorted, "You are a liar! I am no more a witch than you are a wizard;" or, more rarely, one coolly declared, "These may dissemble for aught I know;" "The devil may take any shape;" "I do not know that there are any witches." In the meantime the Judges and their satellites urge the prisoners to confess, as the only means of salvation either in this world or the next, and the girls shriek from incessant attacks by horrid ghosts. They are seized by the throat and strangled till they are black in the face. They are pinched, pierced with pins, knocked down, and heavy specters sit upon their breasts until the young life is nearly crushed from their bodies. This is varied by more appalling incidents. The girls see, not spirits called "from the vasty deep," but specters from the graves of murdered men, women, and children. They come in their winding-sheets, with faces snowy white when they look at the witnesses, but which turn as red as blood when they look upon the accused. These cry mightily for vengeance, threatening Court and witnesses if their wrongs are not redressed by the punishment of the prisoner. To be sure, the Court see none of these. But then the girls—"the poor afflicted"—do, and it is to their honors just as certainly true.

A less terrific exhibition was the prisoner in specter sitting on a beam, at which the specter-sighted witness pointed, and toward which Court and audience gazed, yet beheld nothing. Nor did these audacious ghosts always keep at such respectful distances. They came into the very face of authority, and once the Judge was assured one sat on the table in front of him. His honor struck at it bravely with his sword-cane, breaking the cane but not, so far as we are informed, hurting the specter.

In all this there was no trifling. There was to every one—from the anxious Judges, oppressed by a sense of their responsibility, to the humblest bystander—with a few exceptions, an appalling reality in the whole scene. To the prisoner it carried with it a blasted reputation, a ruined estate, and an ignominious death. Who was responsible?

Let us look at the Judges out of the Court, through the eyes of their friends as well as enemies, and from a point of view affording greater promptings to a charitable judgment than that afforded by their official bearing.

We will first call upon their friends the Mathers—father and son—to speak in their behalf. These eminent ministers were their personal friends, had a large influence in appointing them to office, and in the bringing into existence the special court over which they so fatally presided. They must be allowed to take the stand, and none will have any reason to doubt the sincerity of their testimony.

Cotton Mather speaking, in his "Wonders of the Invisible World," of the Judges in their connection with the witchcraft proceedings, mentions "their heart-breaking solicitude how they might therein best serve God and man. Have there been faults on any side fallen into? Surely they have at worst been but the faults of a well-meaning ignorance."

In his diary he says, "I saw in most of the Judges a most charming instance of prudence and patience; and I know the exemplary prayer and anguish of soul wherewith they had sought the direction of Heaven above most other people, whom I generally saw enchanted into a raging, railing, scandalous, and unreasonable disposition, as the distress increased upon us. For this cause, though I could not allow the principles that some of the Judges espoused, yet I could not but speak honorably of their persons on all occasions; and my compassion upon the sight of their difficulties, raised by my journeys to Salem, the chief seat of the diabolical vexations, caused me yet more to do so."

Writing to a friend in midsummer, 1692, when the witchcraft excitement was fiercer than the dog-star heat, he speaks of the danger that the devil might "serve the Court a trick" by the evidence presented, and adds, "It is of singular happiness that we are blessed with Judges who are aware of this danger."

Again, "Our honorable judges have used, as judges have heretofore done, spectral evidence, to introduce their further inquiries into the lives of the persons accused; and they have, therefore, by the wonderful providence of God, been so strengthened with other evidences, that some of the witch gang have been fairly executed."

He gives the magistrates an indirect but valuable indorsement in his estimate of the accused persons at Salem Village. It is in this style: "The devil exhibiting himself ordinarily as a small black man, has decoyed a fearful knot of proud, forward, igno rant, envious, and malicious creatures to list themselves in his horrid service by entering their names in a book by him tendered unto them."

Soon after the collapse of the witchcraft excitement, Cotton Mather wrote the history, in part, of the trials by the Special Court, in the preface of which he calls the executed persons "malefactors," and refers to the trials as giving occasion for "a pious thankfulness unto God for justice being so far done among us." When Burroughs, Willard, Proctor, Jacobs, and Carrier were hanged, he was present, and said they all died by a righteous sentence. If, therefore, in his judgment, the executed were proved "malefactors," (and if they had not been legally *proved* so he should not, and we think he would not, have called them "malefactors,") and if the trials evinced "justice" being done, then were the judges the right men, in the right place, at the right time.

The book which contains these words which bear so favorably upon the judges, President Mather read and approved before it was printed.

But we must call upon less partial persons to speak of the judges. Brattle, to whom we have before referred, speaking of the judges and spectral evidence, says that they "will by no means allow that any are brought in guilty and condemned by virtue of specter evidence as it is called."

Mr. Willard in his "Some Miscellany Observations," says that the judges say "the devil is in the specter by the person's consent," and "tell us that the devil cannot represent an innocent person doing mischief." And, at the same time, Mr. Willard represents the judges as saying: "We never imprisoned any on mere spectral evidence, or the bare accusation of the afflicted." If they claimed that they never "imprisoned" any on such evidence, we safely infer that they denied ever condemning any to death by such a process.

Mr. Willard regards this claim, as we might suppose, as preposterous. He answers that they might as well insist that they have not "examined any publicly who were before of good reputation." And Brattle says of such avowals: "Whether it is not purely by specter evidences that these persons are found guilty, I leave any man of sense to judge and determine."

Most men "of sense" who read the court records of the trials will, we think, "judge and determine" that every person committed to prison, and every person whose life was taken away, thus suffered by specter evidence alone. But we may consider, though we may not accept, the magistrate's disclaimer.

The facts, then, concerning the magistrates and ministers seem to stand thus: The magistrates believed that the appearance of a person in specter, tormenting the afflicted, was proof of guilt, because possible only by his consent. The ministers believed that such an appearance was not *certain* proof of guilt, because the devil might assume the shape of an innocent person; but they believed this "a rare and extraordinary" occurrence, and that it was especially so "in cases of judicature." They believed specter evidences of "very great use," as they "justly introduce and determine an inquiry." They did not believe in prohibition, but temperance in its use. The judges said, *we are* temperate in this matter; though we believe we *may*, we never *do* condemn on that evidence. *We follow the advice of the ministers*, and *use it as an inquiry only*. The ministers generally, it is evident, accepted this avowal of the judges, as they esteemed it a matter of devout gratitude that "success" had been attained in endeavors by the judges to detect witchcrafts, and such leading men as the Mathers indorsed the "justice" of the ends reached by the methods used.

The truth appears to be this: That while these two prominent classes of actors in the proceedings were conscientiously, and even religiously, endeavoring to discharge their duty in the fear of God, they were overawed and utterly confounded by the phenomena developed from the initiation to the close of the proceedings. Theirs was the error of a credulity for which they must be judged in connection with the age in which they lived, and the popular furor with which they were surrounded.

But it is an error to claim that the ministers

were on one side and the magistrates on the other, whether in matters of opinion or practice concerning the witchcraft proceedings. They differed among themselves considerably in both these respects.

The venerable John Higginson of Salem had the honor of being cried out against by the circle for his want of sympathy with them and what was done by them. The Rev. John Wise, one of the ministers of Ipswich, wrote a petition at his own peril in behalf of the accused, and is said to have been "discerning enough to see the erroneousness of the proceedings from the beginning." The two ministers of Andover stood clear of the whole business. One of them, Rev. Mr. Dane, shared Higginson's honor of being accused. We have seen Mr. Willard's position both in his tract and in his practice at Groton.

Among the magistrates who had a clean record were Governor Phipps and ex-Governor Bradstreet; Nathaniel Saltonstall of Haverhill, who flatly refused to sit on the bench at the trials in the Special Court, returning to his place only when specters had left; and Robert Pike of Salisbury, who at an opportune and critical time wrote to one of the judges a letter in which, with keen logic, he showed the wrong of the whole proceedings.

CHAPTER XXIX.

The "Poor Afflicted."

WE have endeavored to make a candid inquiry into the relation to the sad transactions of our history, borne by those who had prominence in directing them. But the reader's attention, as the scenes presented have passed before him, has been fixed upon the accusers. What are we to think of them? Were their sufferings, and all the dreadful sounds which they heard, and the fearful sights which they saw, real? Or were they skillful deceivers, conscious of the destruction they wrought, but taking a Satanic delight in it? Looking more closely into the strange phenomena developed through and about them, may we not discern a power behind them of which they were, though not the innocent, yet still the deluded and suffering victims?

To enable the reader to see them more fully, we will repeat, from an eye-witness, the story of the beginning of their experience in suffering. Mr. Hale of Beverly, in a history written a few years after the excitement, speaking of the witchcraft actions of Tituba, says: "After this the afflicted persons cried out of the Indian woman named Tituba that she did pinch, prick, and grievously torment them; and that they saw her here and there where nobody else could. Yea, they could tell where she was and what she did when out of their human sight."

Such was their experience, it will be recollected, at the start. We have seen their later and mature sufferings, declarations, and performances. We will pause for a few moments, and hear what other eye-witnesses have to say about them, and gather the opinions of those living in the midst of the storm which they, in part, raised.

The opinion concerning them of, perhaps, the larger number of the ministers, may be gathered from their uniform phraseology when referring to them in their official and private letters. "Our poor neighbors," "the poor afflicted," "these afflicted children," are constantly recurring phrases.

The magistrates, sitting as Judges in court, regarded their sufferings, sights, and testimonies as simple verities, however they might deceive themselves concerning the use they made of them in their verdicts. Yet we have seen that in some cases, at least, they both saw and acknowledged that the afflicted lied.

Mr. Willard in his tract gives us instructive intimations that "the common vogue," in referring to them, is to say, "that they are scandalous persons, liars, and loose in their conversation, and therefore not to be believed." But he allows that the judges declared that such talk was a mistake. Again he declares them to be "possessed persons;" and that this the Judges "stiffly deny."

We have given, in another place, his reasons in detail for not regarding them as "competent witnesses."

Brattle, one of our best authorities, says of "the afflicted" that they "hold conference with the devil, and are therefore not to be believed." He says, "Good spirits will not lie. But those that speak by these persons have been proved liars, and are, therefore, evil spirits." "The devil," he thinks, "imposes upon their brain, and deludes their fancy and imagination."

Brattle, therefore, very naturally expresses great surprise that they should be "so much countenanced" and consulted—"that the justices," whom he thinks "are well-meaning men," "should so far give ear to the devil, as merely upon his authority to issue their warrants and apprehend people."

Again he says, "The consulting these afflicted, as above said, seems to me to be a very gross evil, a real abomination, not fit to be known in New England, and yet is a thing practiced, not only by *Tom* and *John*—I mean the ruder and more ignorant sort—but by many who profess high, and pass among us for some of the better sort. This is that which aggravates the evil, and makes it heinous and tremendous; and yet this is not the worst of it, for, as sure as I now write to you, even some of our civil leaders and spiritual teachers, who, I think, should punish and preach down such sorcery and wickedness, do yet allow of, encourage, yea, and practice, this very abomination."

He further remarks of these afflicted, or, as he

calls them, "blind and nonsensical girls," that though "they have scores of fits in a day, yet in the intervals of time are hale and hearty, robust and lusty, as though nothing had afflicted them."

We find this same remark concerning the good bodily condition of the girls, made by other writers of the times. The indictments against the accused, after reciting the "detestable witchcrafts" practiced by them upon the bodies of the afflicted whose names are specified, says, that by them "they were and are consumed, pined, and wasted." The chief Judge, however, in charging the first jury, "told them that they were not to mind whether the bodies of the said afflicted were really pined and consumed, as was expressed in the indictment; but whether the said afflicted did not suffer from the accused such afflictions as naturally *tended* to their being pined, consumed, and wasted. This, said he, is a pining and consuming in the sense of the law."

This "robust and lusty" condition of the circle accounts for their good spirits behind the screen, and the necessity of their having "some sport."

The Pastors of Andover, to whose good record we have referred, Messrs. Dane and Barnard, in writing to the Governor and General Court in behalf of their arrested and imprisoned parishioners, boldly stigmatize the accusers as "distempered persons," "children and others who are under a diabolical influence;" they call their declarations "scandalous reports" which they have "got up;" they pronounce the specter evidence "conceit," and that the devil had obtained a great advantage of the authorities, and that many innocent persons were accused and imprisoned.

No doubt there were many in humbler stations who entertained the same opinion of the afflicted. We have already given John Proctor's opinion of them, and his method of curing their distemper. Edward Bishop, attending at one time the trials, was in company at the inn of an "afflicted" Indian. Bishop undertook his cure, as Solomon proposes to reform unruly children. The Indian's condition immediately improved, and he mounted a horse behind a friend to ride home, Bishop being on horseback and riding beside them. On the way the Indian had one of the afflicted person's "amazing fits," and laid hold of his companion with his teeth. Bishop applied to him the rod, and "he soon recovered and promised not to do so any more." The result led Bishop to declare that he believed he could cure all the afflicted in the same way; but this remedy was in advance of the times, and Bishop soon found himself, as many progressive men have, in prison for his truly excellent discovery.

Joseph Putnam, father of Israel of Bunker Hill fame, turned his back from the first, in contempt, upon "the afflicted," and their patronizing friend, Mr. Parris. Of course, he expected to be cried out against, and he proved equal to the emergency. He kept some one of his horses under saddle night and day. He armed himself and family, and defied the prosecutors. They knew the man, that with him accusation and attempted arrest meant war. He would fight first, and when overpowered, flee. He was not molested.

Such were some of the contemporaneous opinions and feelings existing in reference to the afflicted. That which was unfavorable was exceptional, of course, or there would have been no witchcraft history to write. The phenomena developed in connection with their testimony utterly confounded all, whatever they thought of their character, or the proper method of dealing with them; and there were men in their company, and watching them for months, whose integrity as witnesses could not easily be excelled, and whose intellectual sagacity was of the first order. All the Putnams were men, as we have seen, of independent thought and observation, and without fear in uttering their convictions. Deacon Ingersoll's conscientious and prayerful watching saw no trick. Some of the judges, and all of the attending ministers, were educated men, trained to a keen discernment, but they could see no legerdemain—no cunning acting, or sham pretensions on the part of the girls.

"Joseph Hutchinson," says Mr. Upham, "was a sharp, stern, and skeptical observer." So, doubtless, were many in the attending daily crowds. Yet the opinion was nearly unanimous, that the condition of the accusers was supernatural. Among those who attempted to explain their condition, there was of course a difference of opinion. The judges, with the majority, believed they were "bewitched," that is, afflicted by the devil through the agency of the witches who had volunteered their services for this purpose. Others, with Mr. Willard, believed they were "possessed," that is, under the influence of the devil, without the responsibility of any out of themselves. To this last conclusion we are as much bound now as any were then—bound to it by the credible accounts of the experience of these girls and other "afflicted," and by the similarity of such experience to that of many in all ages before and in every generation since, extending, in some degree, down to our own time; and, especially, by their identity in character with the New Testament "possessions." The assumption of trick and practiced performing does not meet the case. There are in it things too deep and difficult for that explanation. God did not work such deeds of darkness. Unaided human power could not. "Looking at these facts as they are, do they not indicate something besides random shots? Does not the curtain seem to conceal a chief actor?"

"The tempest that springs suddenly out of a dead calm, tearing the sea from its foundations and flinging it against the skies, must have a powerful cause somewhere; seen or unseen, a cause there must be. The frightful heaving of a burning volcano must be produced by an existing force. So also must this spiritual earthquake, the frightful sea of evil passions, which surges about and sometimes threatens to engulf us, be produced by a power not figurative but literal. Actual force in a living spirit, as the psychological root, becomes an absolute necessity.

"The possibility of Satanic agency in spiritualism we base upon the Bible. It speaks unqualifiedly of demoniacal possession, though it does not tell us what it is; of witchcraft without describing it; of necromancy without offering explanations; and of those having familiar spirits, without disclosing their origin—whether they are from earth or hell." *

The responsibility of the afflicted for this possession by the devil we will not attempt to measure. It is enough to say that it must have been fearfully great. It is seen in part, in the occasion which they gave him thus to enter them. They did not obey the Divine injunction which commands us to "resist the devil." They drew near to him, in the nightly performances of their circle, as their modern successors do, and he drew near to them. They sought him in endeavoring to pry into the forbidden secrets of the spirit-world, and they were found of him with terrible power. They resisted God when they approached the devil by their nightly performances; they cast off his Spirit, whose office work it is to draw the mind and heart away from these intermeddlings; they despised the declarations of his Word, which forbids all such practices. This is the great moral lesson of our story. Let the young learn by it to avoid the "circles." Let them listen to the commands given by God ages ago, and which have never been re-

* "Credo."

voked: "Regard not them that have familiar spirits, neither seek after wizards; . . . I am the Lord your God." Lev. xix, 31. "And the soul that turneth after such as have familiar spirits, and after wizards, . . . I will even set my face against that soul, and will cut him off from among his people." Lev. xx, 6.

Concerning the later history of the most of the afflicted we know nothing. The black cloud of infamy rests upon their name. In an act of the Legislature of the Province, which removed the stain given by the law to their victims, this sentence occurs: "Some of the principal witnesses and accusers, in those dark and severe prosecutions have since discovered themselves to be persons of profligate and vicious conversation." Of the few who had a better subsequent record we shall speak in our pleasanter task of portraying the *penitential tears* which were shed.

CHAPTER XXX.

Penitential Tears.

THE sudden subsiding of the witchcraft delusion in the autumn of 1692, and its almost entire extinction during the following winter and spring, implied not only an opening of the eyes of the people in reference to the accusers, but an awakened tenderness toward the accused. We are therefore prepared for acknowledgments of mistakes made, halting confessions of wrong done, or heart-felt contrition, and penitential tears, on the part of the actors in the tragedy, according as they see their responsibility for its terrible results, and desire squarely to meet it in a Christian manner. We shall endeavor, in a brief chapter, to portray the development of this feeling. It will be a pleasant task; and if the penitence shall not be found as general nor as deep as the case plainly requires, we may find occasion for charity in the greater readiness of our own hearts to condemn sin in others, than to see and confess it ourselves.

We will begin with the ministers—with some of them who were most deeply involved in responsibility.

The Rev. Mr. Hale of Beverly stood, during those terrible months when the arrows of death were being shot into many families, in close affinity to the hands which drew the bow. Any confession, therefore, from him will be gladly received by the reader—the more frank and earnest, the more satisfactory, of course. In his book, written soon after the delusion, he says:

"I would come yet nearer to our own times, and bewail the errors and mistakes that have been made in the year 1692, by following such traditions of our fathers, maxims of the common law, and precedents and principles, which now we may see, weighed in the balance of the sanctuary, are found too light. Such was the darkness of the day, the tortures and lamentations of the afflicted, and the power of former precedents, that we walked in the clouds and could not see our way. I would humbly propose whether it would not be expedient that somewhat more should be publicly done than yet hath for clearing the good name and reputation of some that have suffered upon this account."

In another place he proceeds to state, in six particulars, "Wherein it doth appear that there was a-going too far in this affair." He then in effect acknowledges that some innocent persons had been executed.

Cotton Mather copied into his "Magnolia" with approval, and thus indorsed, these six proofs that there had been a-going too far. This is the only confession that we find from him of "errors and mistakes," or "a-going too far," in which he was so deeply involved.

The Rev. John Higginson, to whom we have

referred as having a good record, senior Pastor of the Church in Salem, wrote a preface to Mr. Hale's book. He was then eighty-two years old. He says the publication of the book will be timely and useful, among other reasons: "That whatever errors or mistakes are fell into in the dark hour of temptation that was upon us may be (upon more light) discovered, acknowledged, and disowned by us, as that it may be matter of warning and caution to those who come after us, that they may not fall into the like. 1 Cor. x, 11."

He proceeds to suggest that the law set forth in Leviticus, fourth chapter, requiring a sin-offering for the sins of ignorance committed by the rulers and congregation, is binding "upon us in a Gospel way."

From no persons will it be more gratifying to receive the evidence of penitential tears than from the Rev. Mr. Parris of the Village, and the Rev. Mr. Noyes of Salem town. We present such facts bearing in that direction as we have.

In November, 1694, about two years after the collapse, Mr. Parris's parish difficulties revived, with new and bitter elements of discord. To the complaints of earlier months were added those growing out of his connection with the trials of the accused. Their friends, among whom John Tarbell and Samuel Nurse, son-in-law and son of Rebecca Nurse, were prominent, urged their complaints with a strong will and skillful management. Closely pressed in the conflict, he read to his opponents a paper entitled "Meditations for

Peace," from which the following confessions are an extract: "In that the Lord ordered the late horrid calamity, which afterward, plague-like, spread in many other places, to break out first in my family, I cannot but look upon as a very sore rebuke, and humbling providence, both to myself and mine, and desire so we may improve it.

"In that also in my family were some of both parties, namely, accusers and accused, I look also upon as an aggravation of the rebuke, as an addition of wormwood to the gall.

"In that means were used in my family (though totally unknown to me or mine, except servants, till afterward) to raise spirits, and create apparitions, in no better than a diabolical way, I do look upon as a further rebuke of Divine Providence. And by all, I do humbly own this day, before God and his people, that God has been righteously spitting in my face. (Numbers xii, 14.) And I desire to lie low under all this reproach, and to lay my hand upon my mouth."

He further says, that in the management of the witchcraft cases he erred with regard to the use of specter evidence, and the use of one afflicted person to ascertain who afflicted another. He closes by declaring: "I do most heartily, fervently, and humbly beseech pardon of the merciful God, through the blood of Christ, of all mistakes and trespasses in so weighty a matter; and also all your forgiveness of every offense in this and other affairs, wherein you see or conceive I have erred and offended; professing in the presence of Almighty God, that what I have done has been, as for substance as I apprehended was duty, however through weakness, ignorance, etc., I may have been mistaken."

"The elders and messengers of the Churches," who met in council at Salem Village, April, 1695, in reference to Mr. Parris' difficulties with his parish, declare that he had taken, in the witchcraft matters, "Sundry unwarrantable and uncomfortable steps;" but they advise, since "by the good hand of God" he had been brought to see his error and to "fully express it," "that a Christian charity may and should receive satisfaction therewith."

Dr. Bentley says of Mr. Noyes that "He came out and publicly confessed his error, never concealed a circumstance, never excused himself; visited, loved, blessed the survivors whom he had injured; asked forgiveness always, and consecrated the residue of his life to bless mankind."

A little later than the date of the confession of Mr. Parris, twelve ministers of Essex County petition the General Court in behalf of those who had suffered in name and estates by the witchcraft proceedings; they call the accusers "young persons under diabolical molestations;" confess that innocent persons had suffered by credit given to them; and "that God may have a controversy with the land on that account."

About the same time an eminent minister of Malden wrote to the president of Harvard College, declaring the great errors of 1692, that innocent blood had been shed, and that "public and solemn acknowledgement of it, and humiliation for it," is a duty; and that the more "particularly and personally" it is done the more pleasing it would be in the sight of God, and the more effectual in turning away his wrath.

The jurors, by whose verdict the nineteen persons were condemned to death in the Special Court, caused to be published a frank, Christian confession of the great wrong that had been done through them. They did, in fact, but act in accordance with the law and evidence, as interpreted and enforced by the Chief-Justice; yet they became painfully affected by the recollection of what they had done as jurors, and the confession which follows was the result. After speaking of the specter evidence which they were prevailed upon to accept, and of their own ignorance of such matters, and the innocent blood which had been shed thereby, they say: "We do therefore signify to all in general, and to the surviving sufferers in special, our deep sense of and sorrow for our errors in acting on such evidence in the condemning of any person; and do hereby declare, that we justly fear that we were sadly deluded and mistaken, for which we are much disquieted and distressed in our minds, and do therefore humbly beg forgiveness, first, of God for Christ's sake, for this our error, and pray that God would not impute the guilt of it to ourselves nor others; and we also pray that we may be considered candidly and aright by the living sufferers, as being then under the power of a strong and general delusion, utterly unacquainted with, and not experienced in matters of that nature.

"We do heartily ask forgiveness of you all, whom we have justly offended; and do declare, according to our present minds, we would none of us do such things again, on such grounds, for the whole world; praying you to accept of this by way of satisfaction for our offense, and that you would bless the inheritance of the Lord, that he may be entreated for the land."

The General Court, as the representative organ of the whole people, was slow in shedding the becoming tears of penitence. They first ordered a day to be observed for public humiliation, fasting, and prayer, in reference to the sins committed in the "late awful tragedy;" with tardiness they removed the legal stains upon the names of the condemned; with greater seeming reluctance they acknowledged their responsibility for the spoliations by the officers of the law of the property of the accused, and made a late, insufficient, and unjustly divided appropriation to meet the demands of restitution.

The first Church in Salem, which had excommunicated, under the most painful circumstances, Rebecca Nurse and Giles Corey, "crossed and blotted out," in 1712, the records of excommunication against them.

The Salem Village Church was more prompt and explicit in their acts of reparation and their expressions of sorrow. In 1702 they rescinded the act of excommunication against Martha Corey, declaring that it was done without sufficient evidence of her guilt, and that her exclusion from the Church "was not according to the will of God."

We are most happy to be able to include at least one of the judges in our account of those who felt and publicly acknowledged their sins in the witchcraft matters. Judge Sewall of Boston was by no means the most deeply involved in guilt, but his contrition was eminently Christian. On the general fast-day he rose before the whole congregation, in the Old South Church in Boston, of which he was a member, and handed the Pastor his written confession. It expressed his grief at the part he took in the witch trials; begged forgiveness of God and the people, and requested their prayers for himself and for the guilty State. He remained standing while the paper was being read. He observed annually in private during the remainder of his life a day of humiliation and prayer, as an expression of his abiding sense of the great wrong which he had done.

Whittier thus embalms in verse this beautiful incident:

"Stately and slow, with thoughtful air,
His black cap hiding his whitened hair,
Walks the Judge of the great Assize,
Samuel Sewall, the good and wise.
His face with lines of firmness wrought,
He wears the look of a man of thought,
Who swears to his hurt and changes not;
Yet touched and softened, nevertheless,
With the grace of a Christian gentleness,
The face that a child would climb to kiss!

True and tender, and brave and just,
That man might honor and women trust.
   Touching and sad, a tale is told,
Like a penitent hymn of a psalmist old,
Of the fast which the good man life-long kept,
With a haunting sorrow that never slept,
As the circling year brought round the time
Of an error that left the sting of crime,
When he sat on the bench of the witchcraft courts,
With the laws of Moses and Hale's Reports,
And spoke in the name of both the word
That gave the witch's neck to the cord,
And piled the oaken planks that pressed
The feeble life from the warlock's breast!
All the day long, from dawn to dawn,
His door was bolted, his curtains drawn;
No foot on his silent threshold trod,
No eye looked on him save that of God,
As he baffled the ghosts of the dead with charms
Of penitent tears, and prayers, and psalms;
And with precious proofs from the sacred word
Of the boundless pity and love of the Lord,
His faith confirmed and his trust renewed
That the sin of his ignorance sorely rued,
Might be washed away in the mingled flood
Of his human sorrow and Christ's dear blood!

We have stated that the historic record of the afflicted persons is, in general, that their subsequent life proved them to be "vile varlets," and utterly without credit. We are happy to find that this statement was not true of all. Ann Putnam, whose position among the accusers we have seen to be that of chief actor and spectral sight-seer, may be classed among those who shed tears of penitence. Her parents, who were largely responsible for their daughter's conduct, died quite near to each other, in 1699. She was then nineteen years of age; a large number of children, all younger than herself, were left in her care. Her health was feeble, and she soon became an invalid. A faithful Pastor, in whom the Village Church and parish were perfectly united, gently led her to a knowledge of Christ by faith in his atonement. She desired to make a public profession of this faith, and at the same time, to make an equally public confession of her sense of the wrong she had done in the great tragedy. Her confession was written, recorded in the church books, and signed by her. On the 25th of August, 1706, the day appointed for her public confession, a great concourse of people gathered at the Village Church. There must have been sad and suggestive recollections of the gatherings to witness her supposed mental and bodily agonies, and to hear her frightful shrieks and wild ravings against the prisoners. Both the crowd and the object of their interest were now in their right minds. The Pastor, Mr. Green, read the confession, while Ann stood, and, at its close, acknowledged it to be hers. She then gave some account of her conversion, and was received into the Church. It was doubtless a solemn and profitable day.

She confessed that innocent blood had been shed by her testimony and that of others; that she was deluded by the devil; that she felt deep sorrow, desired to be humbled and to lie in the dust, especially for being the chief instrument in accusing

Rebecca Nurse and her two sisters. She finally begs forgiveness of God, and of all those to whom she had given sorrow or offense. She affirmed that she had never testified against any through ill-will. She never confessed that tricks or fraud of any kind had been used by herself or the other girls.

She died in 1716, about thirty-six years of age. Her will, made toward the close of life, breathes an abiding confidence in the cleansing blood of Christ. She had greatly sinned, but her penitential tears seem to have been sincere, her faith genuine, and the blotting out of her sins was "as a thick cloud."

CHAPTER XXXI.

A Visit to the Historic Localities.

WE have told the story of the Salem witchcraft. We have endeavored to make the reader acquainted in some measure with the people among whom it occurred. We have introduced them to some of the principal sufferers, and tried candidly to present material by which the responsibility of the principal actors may be estimated, glancing for this purpose at the later history and confessions of a few of them, that they might speak, on this point, for themselves.

The impression made by the facts thus presented may be deepened by a visit to the most prominent localities where they occurred. Fortunately we shall follow a pains-taking guide, who has left nothing to be investigated which affords a probability of additional information in reference to them. We shall find the people every-where ready to enter into the object of our visit upon the slightest intimation of it, for, as they remark, "Mr. Upham has been here for the same purpose a great many times." With the map accompanying his History in hand, and remembering the descriptions given of the localities, a stranger may find any place. It is not often that an investigator into an important historic period provides the means of so perfect a reproduction of its scenes.

On leaving the cars at the station of the Eastern Railroad, Salem, we are quite near points of interest. The station-house fronts Washington-street, and the track of the road has been tunneled under its center across the city. Walking up the street on the right-hand side, a few rods, to the corner of Essex-street, we stand before the First Church. Its marble tablets tell the principal facts in the history of its site. Here was the meeting-house in which some of the preliminary trials of the witches took place. It was "a great and spacious house," and it was within its walls that "a demon, invisibly entering, tore down a part of it," as Bridget Bishop, passing on her way from the jail to the court-house, "gave a look toward the house." The present building is very substantial, and evidently has never been so abused.

Directly opposite the church was the residence of Judge Hathorne.

Crossing Essex-street, and keeping along Washington-street to the corner of Church-street, we are near the site of Bridget Bishop's house. About its orchard, and in through the closed doors and windows of the neighbors' houses, if we may believe witnesses, she played in specter some very naughty pranks. Directly opposite was the residence of the Rev. Mr. Noyes, her Pastor, and her deluded prosecutor. Bridget, it will be recollected, moved from the town into the extreme eastern part of the Village some years before her execution.

In the middle of Washington-street, near where Church and Lynde streets now enter it, is the site of the Court-house in which, after Court and jurors had been overawed by specters, the accused received their death sentence. There is now a continual roar of railroad cars beneath its old foundation, thundering the admonition of modern civilization in the ears of any old fogy specter who might wish to enter the new Court-house, a few rods distant.

Passing through Federal-street to St. Peter's-street—the old Prison Lane—and turning a few steps to the left, on the western side, we face the site of the old jail, where, with many other victims of the delusion, the Rev. George Burroughs was chained at the end of his forced and rapid journey from Maine. The new jail near the same spot, with its ample grounds and well-ordered surroundings, bears evidence that ministers of the Gospel are not likely to find lodgings in its cells by a surprisal and on the testimony of shadowy witnesses. This new jail overlooks a burial-ground; somewhere not far from this, according to tradition, Giles Corey suffered the penalty of keeping his mouth closed when the Court demanded, "Guilty or not guilty?" There was, for many years, a superstition in the minds of visionary people that Corey's specter haunted the field where the deed was done; and boys of the "olden time," as they played in the vicinity, sung a ditty beginning with these lines:

"'More weight! more weight!'
Giles Corey cried."

"As for that night," (it must have been in the *night*,) in which it was said that such a deed was done, "let darkness seize upon it; let it not be joined unto the days of the year; let it not come into the number of the months."

Leaving the vicinity connected with so many painful associations, passing through St. Peter's-street to Essex-street, then turning to the left, we come, after a few moments' walk, opposite No. 65, on the south side. The yellow-colored two-story house before us, standing end to the street, not marked now by any peculiar antique character, is the "Beadle Tavern" of 1692. Some additions have been made on the eastern side, and the hand of modern innovation, no doubt, has touched it since the "old man with two crutches"—George Jacobs, Sen.—and many others, stood in one of its rooms, face to face with "authority," and were commanded to tell "who afflicts these poor afflicted." It is not large now, and must have been smaller then, so that no great crowd could have witnessed the exciting scene, and on this account it must have been a better place for the examinations than "the great meeting-house," or the more ample Court-house.

There is much more of interest, in the city, connected with the object of our visit, but the reader may be impatient to accompany us to localities in and about the Village. Taking the cars on the Salem and Lowell Railroad, and stopping at the junction with it of the Georgetown and Boston Railroad, we are on the farm, five miles from Salem, which Giles Corey owned, and on which he had lived thirty years when the witchcraft storm swept over it. His three hundred acres spread out from the center near which the depot now stands. With the map and the accompanying description in our hands we readily found the site of his house, a few rods from where we stepped from the cars, on a rising ground west of the Lowell Railroad track. It is such a spot as an experienced pioneer would select. It is surrounded by a fine variety of swamp, meadow, and upland. We tried to reproduce Longfellow's poetic conception of it. "The tall poplar-trees" had, with their owner, moldered into dust. "The house, the barn, the orchard and the well," had disappeared. But here was, "The pleasant landscape stretching to the sea." Beneath our feet was the foundation, and some of the broken bricks of the chimney of his house.

Wishing to assure ourself that we had selected the right spot, we entered into conversation with a man who was chopping wood near by. It proved to be the present owner, Mr. Benjamin Taylor. Seeing us with pencil and paper in hand, he readily guessed our errand. He was quite free to converse on the subject which interested us. He remarked, "I saw you standing upon the very site of the old Corey house." His father purchased the place about eighty years ago. The swell of land on which Corey lived Mr. Taylor's father had not esteemed worth cultivating. But about twenty years ago his son put in the plow and turned up the foundation stones, and pieces of brick of the old style. The plowshare disturbed among the rubbish a large black-snake. There were no "afflicted persons" now to see in it the "imp" of a wizard, or Mr. Taylor's plowing might have proved a disastrous business. As it was, the snake lost his head by the plowshare, and the spot bore a good harvest.

A spoon and a pair of scissors were turned up as mementoes of its first owner. Mr. Taylor suggested that the spoon was that with which Corey ate his bean-porridge. It is of the oldest style, its bowl round, and its handle end headed up like the head of a nail.

A school-house, of fine architectural construction and furnishing, lately dedicated, stands upon one portion of the Corey estate. This, with the clatter of neighboring woollen mills, and the whistle of the steam-engine from four points of the compass, give assurance of the progress the neighborhood has made since Corey died a horrible death to save it from legal spoliation.

We took the cars back to Peabody Square—"The Middle Precinct"—and then, "minding to go afoot"—the best way of traveling when visiting historic localities—we took the road to the Iron Works on Endicott River. A few rods from the bridge, on the south side of the river, is the

George Jacobs' farm. We had the satisfaction here of seeing, not merely the site of his house, but the house itself, a sober, venerable, and substantial building, unmarred by modern improvements. It has always been in the Jacobs family. The present owner and occupant is the last of six sons, among whom his father divided one hundred and twenty acres, the homestead falling to him with twenty acres, all that is now owned by the Jacobs' name of the original farm. We found Mr. Jacobs very courteous, showing us the interior of the house, even to the attic, where the size of the chimney in the center of the hewn oaken timbers could be seen. It faces the south, and the present owner added, many years ago, a lean-to with a chimney to the north side, which seems to be the only change ever made in its outward appearance. It is beautifully situated on land rising gently from the river to a height which commands a view of river, town, and country. The grave of George Jacobs, the only one certainly known among the victims of the spectral condemnations, is a few rods from the house, on a spot from which the land descends to the water. In Mr. Jacobs' recollection it was on the edge of a grove, and was overshadowed by a fine old oak. Tradition says that a young grandson obtained the body at the place of execution, strapped it on the back of a horse, brought it to the farm, and buried it in this place. The remains were exhumed in 1864, and found to answer in all respects to the accounts of his age and size. They were redeposited in the

The Townsend Bishop House.

same place with reverent care. The field in which they lie having passed from the Jacobs family, the stones which long designated the grave have been removed to make way for the plow, which turned up the soil last year for an onion bed. The spot should be purchased and inclosed by lovers of historic landmarks.

Mr. Jacobs knew well his grandmother, who was born in 1725, and lived to a great age. She lived in this house from her marriage to her death. It is a singular fact that she is not known to have talked of the tragedy connected with the family, nor to have related any incidents of the witchcraft proceedings, though she must have been conversant with some witnesses of its scenes. It confirms the truth of Mr. Upham's remark, that the people of that period, and their children, regarded the subject as one to be blotted from remembrance as soon and as perfectly as possible.

We passed over the Endicott River bridge, and turned off from the main road into the grounds of the "Orchard Farm" of Governor Endicott. A portion of them are owned to-day by his descendants bearing his name. We looked at the famous pear-tree planted by the Governor, and perhaps brought over from England by him on his first voyage. It is undoubtedly "the oldest inhabitant" of its family.

With our face turned toward Danvers Center—"Salem Village"—we were soon on the "Townsend Bishop" farm, the owner of which, with owners of adjoining farms, contended so successfully, and, as we think, so wrongfully with the owner of the "Orchard Farm." The house built by Townsend Bishop still stands, with a remarkably green old age. It has a marvelous history! We have related the facts connected with it in the course of our story. Its chief interest to us is in the fact that it was long the home of Rebecca Nurse, and that from it, in her old age, she went out to suffer her great wrong. Its identity is clearly established. Francis Nurse, husband of Rebecca, after her death, gave up the homestead to his eldest son, Samuel, who immediately took possession. The rest of the property he divided among his four sons and four daughters. The children who live in it to-day are the direct descendants of Rebecca Nurse. Some slight additions have been made to it, and it has probably always been kept in good repair. Its hewn oaken timbers are equal to the friction of another century. It is surrounded by the variety, so desirable to the early settlers, of high land, and that more readily used for grazing. It will be remembered that after Francis Nurse bought the estate, his sons and sons-in-law cut from the forest within his claim farms on which they erected houses. The house of his son Samuel, and that of Tarbell, his son-in-law, still remain. Tarbell's must have been a first-class house in its day, but is now dilapidated and unoccupied. It was made a condition of sale by the father that the houses of the children should be connected with the homestead by well-opened driveways. As we looked upon the relation to each other of these estates, and their pleasant location, we felt, as never before, the terribleness of the shock of the witchcraft visitation to their early owners.

It has been the uniform tradition of the family that the body of Rebecca Nurse was obtained, and deposited by her family in the family burying-ground upon the estate.

A walk of little less than a mile from the Townsend Bishop house brought us into the place where the tragic scenes of our story commenced—Salem Village. Under its present name, Danvers Center, and in its present aspect, a more inviting locality could hardly be found. Intelligence, thrift, and comfort are every-where apparent. Under the guidance of Mr. Moses Prince, who has been called "an embodiment of the history, genealogy, and traditions of the vicinity," we readily found what we wished to see. The first site visited was that of the parsonage in which the witchcraft delusion was cradled. The spot seemed dreary and forbidding. Perhaps it was the wintry day of our visit which induced the impression. The land about it looked as if it was now little cared for, and little worth caring for. It is away from the present street, and none of the modern houses have sought this place. A few broken bricks are all that mark the place where the parsonage stood. It was a good-sized house for those days, "forty-two feet in length, twenty feet broad, thirteen feet stud," having "no gable end," but "a lean-to." It was becoming for the notorious house to return to dust, and it is also fitting that the spot should be deserted.

Quite near the parsonage, but on higher and better ground, stood the house of Jonathan Walcot, father of Mary Walcot, who will be remembered as an original member of the circle. Mr. Prince remarked that he plowed up, at one time, some of the bricks of the chimney. This spot too is forsaken.

We walked down to the site of the old meeting-house, now occupied by a large farm-house. The lane leading to it, through which the frenzied crowds poured to witness the bewildering transactions in the church, has shared the blight resting upon many other historic localities of the witchcraft period. A lady, brought up in the Village, remarked to us that, when a girl, she had always avoided so far as possible this locality, especially in the evening. The old meeting-house disappeared soon after 1692. It was stripped, moved from the spot, and converted into a barn. Some of the aged people of the present generation remember it in this form, as, bowing under the weight of years and sorrowful memories, it was crumbling to dust. Its successor was built on Watch-house Hill, before Deacon Ingersoll's door, and only a few rods from the old site. Here stands the Village church of to-day, a conspicuous object viewed from the surrounding country. The present parsonage has taken the eligible lot on which was the deacon's residence, whose "great room" was privy to so many witchcraft scenes.

The well-preserved church and parish records form a kind of connecting link between the present and the events we have narrated. We were permitted, by the courtesy of Augustus Mudge, Esq., the parish clerk, to examine those in his keeping. They were begun in 1672. The handwriting is excellent, and the manner in which the facts are stated show considerable practice in composition. They are, in a measure, a journal of the progress of the Village. Many important facts have been gleaned from them by Mr. Upham. It was a stormy time when they were ushered into the world, but they lie placidly beside their fellows of calmer periods.

Turning from the Village, we may take the "Danvers Center and Salem" omnibus, which passes through *Peabody*, which we find it difficult to speak of in this connection except as the "Middle Precinct."

As we enter Salem we may discern a range of rocky hills upon our right hand, rising somewhat abruptly from Boston-street, through which we are riding. Stepping from the omnibus we find a ready guidance from the passers-by to *Witch Hill.** Its top could not have been more barren and drear in 1692 than it is to-day. The population has ascended its northern side, and its eastern declivity, toward Boston-street, is filled with dwelling-houses and places of mechanical labor. The hill descends sharply into a valley on the south side, and somewhat so on the west, and these sides are

* See Frontispiece.

rugged and difficult of access. Just before reaching the Boston and Salem turnpike, a third of a mile south, the rocky range re-appears. About two rods from this southern brow of the hill stood, until within a few years, a venerable tree on which, according to the popular belief, the victims of the witchcraft mania were hanged. Pieces of it are preserved and shown to the curious. Very little vegetation could ever have grown upon the immediate hill. No dwelling is likely to occupy it. But the views from Witch Hill are of almost unsurpassed beauty—views of city, town, and country; of inlets running to the sea, across which bridges have been thrown, displacing the olden "ferries;" of the extended shore line, headlands, islands, and ocean. The rapid flight in and from the city of the eastern railroad train can be followed by the smoke of the engine, and occasional glances of it obtained at the openings of the ledges.

The Frontispiece is a fair representation of Witch Hill. The probable place of the hanging was between what appears to be two flag-staffs. The buildings at the foot of the hill, on the extreme right, indicate the direction of Boston-street. The ascent of the condemned persons was from the rear of the center of the picture.

One of our visits was made on a beautiful summer-like October morning. The atmosphere was clear and the panorama before us delightful. Only about a week earlier in the season the last of the witchcraft victims suffered on this spot. Perhaps it was such a morning. The natural features of the view were as pleasant then as now. Some of them at least saw God as they stood on the ladder, smiling through nature; but more fully, and with a deeper comfort, through his Word, conveying promises of eternal life by a crucified Saviour. We joy to think that such, forgiven and forgiving, felt that the moment, though so solemn and awful, was the best of their lives.

Our more serious thoughts while viewing the scene were interrupted by the approach of an Irishman, who lived near. Guessing the object of our visit, he seemed desirous to enter into conversation. We asked him if there were any witches haunting the hill. With a merry twinkle of his eyes he answered promptly, "Many a one, bewitching the boys!" He meant to say, with all the people of the vicinity, that,

> " *Our* witches are no longer old
> And wrinkled beldames, Satan-sold,
> But young and gay, and laughing creatures,
> With the heart's sunshine on their features;
> Their sorcery, the light which dances
> Where the raised lid unveils its glances."
>
> WHITTIER.

Access to Witch Hill from the street is not easy now, and must have been rough and jolting to the riders "in the cart," of the summer of 1692. As Mr. Upham has suggested that their approach must have been up the north-eastern side, not far from Aborn-street, we, at one time, walked from the site of the old jail, along the route taken by the sheriff with the condemned in charge, ascending the hill in that direction. It is a moderate walk of thirty-five minutes. With the cart occasionally "getting set," the poor victims very likely dragged through an hour.

From the pleasant summit of Witch Hill, with its sad memories pressing upon our minds, we bid the reader adieu. As we take the hand of our young friends we would whisper again in their ears the lesson of our story, "Resist the devil;" approach him not in the circles of those with whom he is familiar, as did the girls of our history; nor by any other wicked acts or unholy thoughts give place to his influence. Resist him, and he will flee from you. "Draw near to God, and he will draw near to you."

www.ingramcontent.com/pod-product-compliance
Lightning Source LLC
LaVergne TN
LVHW020231110826
845151LV00003B/887

* 9 7 8 1 4 2 5 5 3 2 3 5 2 *